CLAREN.

MW00795534

Edited by

PAUL CRAIG

CLARENDON LAW SERIES

COMPETITION LAW AND ANTITRUST

A Global Guide

DAVID J. GERBER

Distinguished Professor of Law
Chicago-Kent College of Law

OXFORD
UNIVERSITY PRESS

Great Clarendon Street, Oxford, OX2 6DP,
United Kingdom

Oxford University Press is a department of the University of Oxford.
It furthers the University's objective of excellence in research, scholarship,
and education by publishing worldwide. Oxford is a registered trade mark of
Oxford University Press in the UK and in certain other countries

Published in the United States of America by Oxford University Press
198 Madison Avenue, New York, NY 10016, United States of America

British Library Cataloguing in Publication Data
Data available

Library of Congress Control Number: 2020934577

ISBN 978–0–19–872747–7 (hbk.)
ISBN 978–0–19–872748–4 (pbk.)

Printed and bound by
CPI Group (UK) Ltd, Croydon, CR0 4YY

This book is dedicated to Eleanor Fox
Who has helped me to view competition law more clearly and broadly

and to the memory of Jerome Bruner
Who helped me to see everything more clearly and broadly

PREFACE

Frequent encounters with three ways of thinking about competition law have led me to write this Guide. They often stand in the way of understanding. And I have often witnessed the harm they cause during many years in the transnational practice of law in the US and Europe, in classrooms, conferences, and lecture halls in many countries, and in studying the development and operation of competition (and antitrust) laws of all kinds and types. These harmful views of competition law obscure many of its important dimensions—what it can do, what it actually does, and what influences decisions. This Guide illuminates these three dimensions.

Accessibility is a central problem. Many who could greatly benefit from understanding more about the subject never even try or soon give up, because they encounter obstacles and confusion in their path. Some assume that it is just too difficult. Others try to understand something about a competition law regime, but abandon the effort when they encounter webs of detail and uncertainty about what competition law regimes do and why. Many are simply unaware of competition law's potential relevance for them—both its threats and its opportunities. Its central purpose is not easy to grasp: law interferes with economic competition in order to protect it? This sounds abstract, but competition laws have very practical consequences! This Guide creates paths around these obstacles—for both those who want to know more about their own competition laws and its consequences and those who want to understand and predict decisions in other regimes.

My strategy is easy to state: focus on what is important and avoid the unnecessary details that often deaden interest and impair access. Competition laws share core elements, and all competition law institutions face similar basic problems and draw tools from the same toolbox to deal with them. The Guide focuses on these core elements and notes patterns of variation on each. This opens doors to understanding what is happening in one's own competition law regime and prepares the way for understanding what to expect in others. Decisions, both formal and informal, provide a key to opening these doors. Focusing on decisions and the influences on them concentrates attention on relevant material and filters out less relevant details. This allows me to keep the Guide short and to provide maximum value to the reader.

Distorted views of competition law are a second source of harm and, for me, frustration and even anguish. Inaccurate beliefs about competition law and its operations mislead and confuse many. They often lead to misunderstanding, mistakes, misunderstood messages, and counterproductive and harmful decisions. For example, many (especially in the US) think of competition law as a technical subject that is just about economics. They conclude that they cannot hope to understand it so they must merely accept the conclusions of "experts." Others see competition law as intended to protect economic interests, but blind to issues of justice and fairness. For some, it is just a facade anyway, so they see little reason to think carefully about it. Many outside the US view it as a form of law created by the US and imposed—or at least urged—on others for the benefit of US business. These and many other images distort views of competition law in harmful ways. Sometimes the images are tinged with innocent arrogance, but at times personal and economic interests lurk behind them. The Guide exposes some of these distortions as well as their sources and the harms they can cause.

A third and often jarring experience has been to note the national blinders that obscure external influences on domestic competition law decisions. Economic activity has become global in scope over the last three decades. Global markets, supply chains, and cross-border investments define much of the world's economy, and competition law is forced to deal with competition law harms in this new environment. Often the competition law of a single country cannot do so effectively, so decision-makers must interact with each other in order to identify and respond to the harms. As a result, domestic decision-makers are subject to influences from other foreign competition law officials, lawyers, and scholars as well as from a myriad of transnational public and private institutions and interests. Yet many talk about domestic decisions without recognizing the web of outside influences that directly or indirectly shape those decisions! They may be aware of some foreign-source pressures and incentives, but they seldom ask how they influence domestic decisions or how they relate to each other.

In response, the Guide provides tools for identifying and assessing foreign influences on domestic decisions. The key here is to recognize that competition law institutions function within a digitally based and interactive global system. It is a new kind of system with its own patterns and rules. Recognizing what the system is and seeing how it works help us identify individual influences and relate these influences to each other, so that we can more clearly see how they exercise their influence.

These strategies together open *doors* into any competition law regime, and they open *windows* for seeing beyond that regime to the outside influences on it.

This is the shortest of my books, but it has demanded much patience and thought. I have long been absorbed by the question "How do I write a book that captures the dimensions of competition law today?" It has to be global in scope because competition law is global in scope, and it must be accessible to anyone anywhere. It should be as condensed as good poetry and as insightful as good judicial decisions. As far as I know, the book is unique. No one has written anything quite like it. I hope that it at least moves toward its goals and helps to encourage others to seek these goals.

ACKNOWLEDGMENTS

My gratitude to all who have improved and supported this project is profound! Above all, as always and forever, my thanks go to Ulla-Britt, my partner and spouse, for her unfailing support of the project (with only an occasional "When is this actually going to be finished?"), for her valuable comments on its contents, and for her limitless willingness to do the little things that have moved it forward.

A list of the others whose help I want to acknowledge is long, and there would be little point in providing all the names (even if I could). I do, however, have to mention a few of them. My Oxford editor, Alex Flach, has provided exceptionally valuable comments on an earlier draft, and he has steadfastly believed in the project's value from its inception. I have been enormously fortunate to work with him. Competition law experts Andre Fiebig, Eleanor Fox, Tadashi Shiraishi, and Spencer Weber Waller have commented on portions of earlier drafts, and I have greatly benefitted from their views. Many workshops, lectures, students, and conversations around the world have provided essential information and insights. I could not begin even to remember all of them, but I have always thanked them, and I hope they will recall those expressions of my gratitude.

Librarians, faculty assistants, and student research assistants at my home institution, Chicago-Kent College of Law, have also been invaluable. I can mention only a few of them. Mandy Lee, a superb research librarian, has been marvelous in finding relevant information and creatively shaping the search for information. Nicole Wagner, an assistant during the last stages of the writing, has been the proverbial "godsend." Her range of talents as librarian, computer specialist, and patient and precise advisor on all things involved in the production of high-quality texts is remarkable. Several excellent student research assistants have also helped along the way. I mention three recent ones who have been especially helpful: Jacob Aleknavicius, Javier Ortega Alvarez, and Samantha Ruben. To say "I couldn't have done it without them" may be trite and overused, but here it is very true and heartfelt.

TABLE OF CONTENTS

1

COMPETITION LAW AND ANTITRUST: A GLOBAL INTRODUCTION AND GUIDE

Economic competition—the battle for profits, money, land, and other resources—is central to the lives of almost everyone almost everywhere. Whether it exists, how intense it is, and how free it is determines the cost of what we buy, whether we have jobs, what kinds of jobs we have, and what opportunities we will have in the future. "Competition law" (also known as "antitrust law") is specifically charged with protecting competition from restraints, so it can have a direct and powerful impact on lives anywhere. The aim of this short book is to make competition law accessible and understandable and to reveal its national and global dimensions.

This type of law increasingly shapes business conduct, influences economic policy, and produces both opportunities and obstacles for people, businesses, and governments across the globe. Should we invest there? Can we sign that contract? Should we develop this project? Can we try this marketing strategy there? What can we do about competitors who use their size and power to block our access to customers? Can technology giants do this with our data? Superficial views and false assumptions can lead a lawyer to advise against a contract that does not pose competition law risks or approve one that is likely to encounter investigations, fines, and even jail sentences. The Guide provides tools for giving everyone better answers to these questions.

Competition law is both domestic and global. Domestic institutions make the decisions that directly affect economic life, but ideas, institutions, and experiences from across the globe often shape those decisions. Each influences the other, so recognizing those influences is often essential for understanding competition law decisions anywhere. It is necessary to grasp the

Competition Law and Antitrust. David J. Gerber, Oxford University Press (2020). © David J. Gerber.
DOI: 10.1093/oso/9780198727477.001.0001

way competition law operates in a particular domestic regime, but it is often equally important to recognize foreign influences on its operation. This Guide is designed for all who want to understand and/or work in this new environment.

National (and sometimes local and regional) laws and institutions are at the center of the picture, so the Guide looks at what they do, how they do it, and why. Competition law regimes everywhere face similar problems and issues, so we examine the features they share. But they respond to them differently, and the Guide highlights the differing responses as well as some of the reasons for them. This strategy directs us to the factors and information that are most likely to be of value to us.

Institutions, individuals, ideas, and experiences from beyond a regime's borders often go unnoticed, because we do not know they might be there or because we do not know why they might be important. Even if we know that these influences might exist, we often do not know where to find them or what consequences they might have. As a result, we misread past decisions and make serious mistakes in predicting what will happen. The Guide enables us to recognize the interplays between national regimes and global forces and make sense of them. This is part of what makes it new, different, and valuable.

Communication is critically important to the interplay of factors that shape decisions, but it is often distorted and undermined by lack of understanding of foreign regimes or biased assumptions about them. These distortions cause lawyers to misunderstand each other, clients to misinterpret what lawyers tell them, and lawyers to misread the requests and expectations of clients. They can also lead officials in one regime to misread messages from their counterparts in another regime, potentially undermining cooperation between them. The Guide's strategies can reduce such mistakes and misunderstandings.

Many wonder what competition law is, why it exists, what it does, and how it operates. Suspicions, thin knowledge, and mistaken assumptions are common not only in the general public, but also among lawyers, public officials, and business leaders. Non-lawyers typically know little or nothing about competition law, and what they think they know is often wrong. Many lawyers have only superficial knowledge of their own competition law and vague and distorted images of other competition laws. Competition law specialists in one country often have spotty and error-filled images of other competition laws and of their influence. The Guide can benefit each of these groups.

A. THE PROJECT

The Guide's central goal is to make competition law more understandable and accessible. Information about competition law—statutory texts, court opinions, and policy statements—is almost limitless and available to anyone with access to the internet. Yet the information is often useless or even misleading unless we know what to look for and how to find it.

A key to doing this is to focus on decisions and ask what factors influence them. Interest in law is almost always about what will happen in the future—that is, what decisions will be made. Yet we often look only at formal evidence of what has happened in the past—for example, statutes and cases. A statute may, for example, state that specified conduct is prohibited, but it may actually have little or no influence on decisions, so its language is likely to lead to bad—perhaps devastatingly bad—decisions. This is particularly likely when we want to know what *foreign* institutions are likely to do. Images of foreign competition laws are inevitably thin and distorted. As a result, we often do not know how information is evaluated and used, and we make assumptions based on biases, ideology, and our own experience. How do we identify what is relevant for interpreting past decisions, predicting future ones, and communicating about it?

The Guide's answer is to see more by looking at less and by knowing where to look. This means highlighting information that is likely to influence relevant decisions and paying less attention to other information. The Guide does not amass details, but instead identifies the information that is most relevant. It presents information and insights that illuminate important and often overlooked factors in competition law decision making. It points to questions that need to be asked and suggests ways of answering them.

B. TOOLS

Questions about law are typically about understanding past decisions or predicting future decisions. This leads to the Guide's focus on *decisions and on the influences that shape them*. Formal decisions are important, but they are shaped by other decisions that give them whatever impact they have. Statutes and cases are important only to the extent that they influence the decisions of people and institutions! That is why the Guide focuses on recognizing and assessing the factors that influence decisions.

Institutions, ideas, and personal relationships shape legal decisions. In our own domestic regimes, we often know much about these factors and how they influence the decisions we want to understand or predict. In contrast, we typically know little or nothing about the influences on decisions in other regimes, so we have no way of assessing their impact or importance. This is why the Guide points us to key factors that influence these decisions.

The influences sometimes come from the domestic regime, but often they come from outside it, so it is critical to recognize how domestic and foreign factors relate to each other. The Guide does this by recognizing the global system in which domestic and foreign individuals, institutions, interests, and power are located and interact. Together the focus on decisions and on the system in which they are embedded enables us to identify high value information and filter out misleading and low value information.

These same tools can also improve communication across borders. Individuals and institutions send messages in order to have they effects they want, and they want to understand the messages they receive. This is not always easy in competition law. Its concepts and principles are often general and abstract. Moreover, competition law language contains a variety of interwoven strands—for example, the native language of a national regime, the regime's professional language (institutions, concepts, etc.), and the language of economics. These factors increase the likelihood that the sender and the receiver of a transborder message will interpret it differently. Many assume that terms have the same meaning across borders, but the assumption can be very misleading and dangerous. The Guide identifies obstacles to communication across borders and ways of avoiding them.

Any reader from any regime can profit from using these strategies. They are meant to be as easy to use as possible, so they can improve anyone's capacity to better understand competition law and to function more effectively in the competition law world. Much study and experience lies behind the strategies, but for you—the reader—the issue is whether they are valuable. I believe that you will find that they are.

C. WHAT THE GUIDE IS NOT

A common image of a "guide" can mislead us, so it is important to clarify what the Guide is not. Many think of a guide as basically a collection of information—for example, a travel guide that gives detailed information about hotels, etc. That kind of guide can be valuable for other purposes, but not here! This Guide is different! It does not amass details; it penetrates them. *It reveals the patterns in the details and thereby makes them more understandable and useful.*

D. OVERVIEW

PART I (Chs. 2–4) clarifies what competition law is and investigates its goals, institutions, and methods.

Chapter 2 examines the identity of competition law. What is it? For a single regime, the question may be relatively easy to answer, but when we widen our view to refer to other regimes, this becomes more difficult. It can create major problems of understanding and communication. The Guide solves these problems by identifying a core meaning that all regimes share and pointing to variations from it. It also reveals some of the forces that shroud competition law's identity.

Chapter 3 looks at competition law's goals. What do governments want these laws to do? Whose interests does competition law serve? We examine stated goals as well as those that may be undisclosed or even intentionally concealed.

Chapter 4 then examines how institutions pursue these goals.

PART II (Chs. 5–7) examines competition law's targets.

What kinds of conduct do competition laws try to deter and how do regimes identify and pursue their targets? The Guide examines the main targets—anticompetitive agreements, dominant firm harms, and mergers. For each it looks at the harms they are thought to cause, the ways in which individual competition laws respond to them, and transborder patterns in the responses.

PART III (Chs. 8–10) looks in some depth at the two most influential competition law regimes—the US and EU—and presents tools for more readily and effectively understanding other competition laws.

Chapter 8 examines US antitrust law, its goals-methods and institution as well as its roles and influence. It is a reference point for discussions of competition law virtually everywhere, and its influence extends in many directions. Ironically, it is also different from other systems in many fundamental ways.

Chapter 9 does the same for competition law in Europe. It is often as influential as its US counterpart, but often for different reasons.

Chapter 10 identifies factors that shape all competition laws and that guide us to relevant information in any competition law regime. It then looks at shaping factors that groups of regimes share and at how we can use them to provide insights into the members of the group. East Asia, Latin America, and emerging markets provide the examples.

PART IV (Chs. 11–12) examines the global system and the changes in competition that challenge both individual regimes and the system as a whole.

Chapter 11 focuses on the interactions among competition law regimes and shows how they constitute a global system. It reviews the formal framework of the system and then looks at how actions, ideas, and influences flow through this system of relationships and shape decisions everywhere.

Chapter 12 looks at two major challenges to competition law—deep globalization and Big Data—and examines how they are changing competition law and challenging its institutions.

E. USES AND USERS

The Guide provides value for many types of users. For those with limited or no knowledge of competition law, it can serve as an introduction, providing points of entry into the ideas, institutions, and language of competition law. For those familiar with some aspects of competition law, it provides information and insights about other aspects of competition law, and for those who know one competition law regime, it provides ways of understanding and dealing with other regimes.

Students will find the Guide invaluable because it identifies basic issues and provides information that they can use in courses on competition law and in related fields such as intellectual property law. It reveals how the details relate to each other and makes the information meaningful—often even exciting.

Legal professionals need to interpret past decisions and predict future ones, and the Guide enables them to perform both tasks more easily, quickly, and effectively. A lawyer may know or suspect that a competition law issue is relevant to the transaction or litigation on which s/he is working, but s/he often does not know how to identify or evaluate it. Confronted with large amounts of information, the legal professional may have few tools for understanding how the pieces fit together. The Guide provides such tools.

Competition law professionals will also find much of value in this Guide. They may know their own laws and even have experience across borders, but the Guide provides them with new perspectives and insights into foreign regimes and into the relationships among competition law regimes. Many will find them valuable.

Officials and Legislators make important decisions about competition law, but they often have limited knowledge of many aspects of the subject and limited interest in the details. The Guide enables them to recognize competition issues and anticipate their potential implications without engaging in prolonged study. In this sense it can serve as a kind of executive summary.

Economists work with economic theory and its applications to economic issues. Often, however, they need to know how a particular competition law regime or group of regimes impacts what they do. The Guide provides insights into the ways in which competition law impacts decisions in these regimes. It enables them to quickly evaluate potential competition law factors and their consequences.

Business people are often unaware of the potential impact of competition law on their companies and their capacity to succeed. This is especially true for those who are located in countries where competition law is weak or nonexistent or where fines are seldom large enough to affect decisions. The Guide enables them to anticipate problems and barriers in their business decisions rather than running into them and sometimes paying a heavy price for doing so. Those caught in competition law's traps tend to be looking for jobs soon thereafter.

Finally, *general readers* may not suspect the ways that competition law influences their daily lives, but they are often very interested in the prices of the goods and services they buy. The Guide shows them how competition laws can affect these elements of their lives. Many are also concerned about how markets produce and distribute wealth. They will acquire here many insights into the role that competition law can play in those areas of social and economic life.

PART I

IDENTITY, GOALS, AND METHODS

2

WHAT IS IT? COMPETITION LAW'S VEILED IDENTITY

The terms "competition law" and "antitrust" mean little, if anything, to most people in most parts of the world. Many have no idea what kind of law it is, and those who believe they know something about it are often wrong. They may have a few pieces of information about the competition law in the country where they live, but seldom more. This is true not only for the general public, but also for many lawyers, officials, and business people. The uncertain identity of competition law is often a major obstacle to clear thinking about it, communicating about it, and making decisions about it.

The obstacles can cause harm within one's own regime, but they are more likely and can cause greater harm when we look across borders. For example, lawyers from the US often assume that other competition laws have the same basic features as antitrust law in the US—that is, that they revolve around economic efficiency goals and that the key decision-makers are courts. Such assumptions are often misleading, hindering the lawyers' efforts to deal with law, lawyers, and clients from other regimes. A related example involves interpreting legal texts from another system. If a lawyer from country A assumes that a competition law statute from country B will be interpreted by reference to economics, but in country B the statute is interpreted by reference to principles of linguistic interpretation, she will completely misread the statute. Inaccurate assumptions also undermine communication. If a lawyer from country A talks to an official in country B about the likely effect of B's competition law on her client, her assumptions may lead her to misinterpret the official's questions and the official to misinterpret her answers. Moreover, each is unlikely to be aware that the other misunderstands their exchange.

Competition Law and Antitrust. David J. Gerber, Oxford University Press (2020). © David J. Gerber.
DOI: 10.1093/oso/9780198727477.001.0001

This chapter examines the identity of competition law. We look at the veils that obscure it, identify a core meaning that can be used everywhere, and review variations among competition law systems.

A. COMPETITION LAW VEILS

Many veils obscure and distort images of competition law. They exist within all systems and influence how competition laws operate and are perceived. Here are some common ones:

1. *Vague goals*: Competition law's goals are abstract. Compare competition law, for example, with laws relating to physical harm to persons. Everyone recognizes the need for laws to protect people from physical harm. Similarly, all recognize the need to protect against fraud and coercion in contracting. In contrast, competition law intervenes in markets in order to protect the way they function. This is not so easy to grasp!

2. *Newness*: In much of the world, competition law is also relatively new. It has played central roles in the US for many decades, but it has become important in other parts of the world much more recently. In some parts of Europe it was little known until the 1990s. In much of the rest of the world, such laws did not even exist until that decade or later, and in some countries they are still not well known. As a result, there has often been little incentive to pay attention to competition law.

3. *Competition law's many shapes and colors*: Variety among competition law systems further clouds its identity. In one country, the term (or its analogue in the local language) may refer to a highly developed set of institutions and legal principles that employ economics to identify and measure economic harm, while in another it may be understood as a form of administrative price control or even a mechanism for reducing economic inequality. Little, it seems, unites them.

4. *Rapid change*: Rapid changes also make it difficult to identify what is fundamental to competition law. For example, US antitrust law changed radically between 1970 and 1990. Its goals were severely narrowed and its methods refocused to

rely primarily on economic effects. Such changes can obscure what has changed, what has stayed the same, and what is fundamental to US antitrust.

5. *Confusion with other areas of law*: Competition law is often confused with other areas of law. For example, many confuse it with unfair competition law, a branch of private law whose principal aim is to *protect competitors* from unfair competitive conduct. This contrasts sharply with the central objective of competition law, which is to *enhance a public good*—namely, effective markets. The distinction has important consequences, but it often goes unnoticed, especially in newer competition law systems.

6. *Politics and ideologies*: Political and ideological agendas can also distort images of competition law. For example, a top US antitrust official not long ago proclaimed that a law could only be called "antitrust (competition law)" if it was based on economic analysis—that is, conformed to the US model. Many outside the US saw the pronouncement as political or ideological or both.

7. *Competition law myths*: Myths obscure competition law. For example, the often-repeated claim that competition law is a US "invention" and that all competition laws derive from it suggests that the US model is "the true" competition law and that deviations from it must be seen as "mistakes" based on lack of understanding or ideology. I and others have shown how fundamentally false and misleading the myth is, but some find it useful, so it persists. As we shall see later, a European version of competition law developed quite independently of US experience—with its own intellectual roots, patterns of thought, and institutional preferences. Its influence has been widespread, particularly among newer competition law systems.

8. *Between public law and private law*: Finally, in the "Civil Law" tradition (i.e., the continental European model and the many systems in Latin America, Asia, and Africa based on it) a sharp division between public and private law can cloud the picture. Especially in continental Europe, private law and public law tend to have separate educational tracks, institutions, values,

and vocabularies. Competition law straddles the two worlds. Each may claim it; each may fear it. When seen as public law, it is often treated as just another form of regulation for the government to use as it wishes. When it is viewed through a private law lens, it often represents a set of principles and institutions for the protection of economic freedom or consumer welfare. The two views often clash.

B. COMPETITION LAW AS A RESPONSE TO A PROBLEM

The terms "competition law" and "antitrust law" refer to a particular type of law, so we need to know what that category includes. The Guide's perspective is global, so the definition cannot be drawn from one country's conception of competition law. Moreover, we cannot rely on the language and vocabulary used in a specific regime. That would lead to endless confusion and often does. Instead we identify the *function* that is at the core of what all or most systems mean by "competition law"—that is, what is the problem?

Any society that relies on markets rather than political control to coordinate economic activity faces a basic problem: The freedom of actors to compete tends to make markets more efficient and increase material benefits to society, but *the same freedom can also be used to restrain competition and undermine these benefits.* Competition law combats these restraints, and the more important the market is to a society's leaders, the more likely it is that they will seek to prevent harm to it. It is best seen as a family of responses to this inherent vulnerability of markets. States can themselves interfere with markets, but that is a very different problem, and we do not deal with it here.

C. A CORE DEFINITION

The Guide uses the terms "competition law" and "antitrust law" to refer to *a general domain of law whose object is to deter private restraints on competitive conduct.* We look more closely at the terms:

1. "General"—The laws included are those that are applicable throughout an economy and thereby provide a framework for all market operations (there are always some exempted sectors). Laws dealing only with specific markets (e.g., telecommunication) do not play that role.

2. "Domain of Law" here refers to a politically authorized set of norms and the institutional arrangements used to enforce them.

Is it law—or is it policy? The relationship between "competition law" and "competition policy" is not always clear. Often the terms are used interchangeably, but there can be important differences between them. Both can refer to norms used to combat restraints on competition, but they represent two different ways of looking at the relevant laws, and the differences can influence how norms are interpreted and applied. "Law" implies that established methods of interpretation are used to interpret and apply the norms and that established procedures are the sole or primary means of enforcing and changing the norms. In this view, the norms are a relatively stable component of a legal system. Thinking of those same norms as "policy," on the other hand, implies that they are a tool of whatever government is in power and that it can use and modify them as it wishes.

3. "Restraint" refers to any limitation imposed by one or more private actors that reduces the intensity of competition in a market.

4. "Competition" refers to a process by which firms in a market seek to maximize their profits by exploiting market opportunities more effectively than other firms in the market.

D. VARIATIONS ON THE THEME

With this function-based core definition in mind, we briefly note here the kinds of variations that exist among competition law systems. The Guide explores the variations more fully in the following chapters.

1. *Goals*: Systems vary according to the objectives they claim to pursue. Some are narrow and technical; others are broad and political or social.

2. *Substantive law*: Most regimes identify the same basic targets (e.g., anticompetitive agreements) but they differ in the extent to which they actually pursue them. Some pursue cartels vigorously and pay relatively little attention to dominant firm conduct. Others focus on vertical restraints or the unilateral conduct of large firms, often reflecting concern over the power of dominant foreign firms.

3. *Institutions*: All competition law systems have at least one public enforcement agency charged with applying competition law's norms. Institutions may look similar on paper, but their capacities, goals, resources, status, and other characteristics vary widely. Some are well-funded and relatively free of interference from political and economic pressures. Well-trained staff follow established procedures to achieve stated goals. Others—many more in number—are poorly funded and strongly influenced by political and/or economic interests.

4. *Procedures and methods*: Procedures and methods also vary widely. Both competition authorities and courts use legal and economic methods in making competition law decisions, but they vary widely in the ways they use them. Moreover, there is great diversity in the procedures used to investigate and enforce the laws.

The following chapters look more closely at the elements of competition law.

3

THE GOALS AND USES OF COMPETITION LAW

Stated goals can guide competition law decisions; they can also obscure them. They can help us interpret and predict decisions, but they can also be misleading. This makes it important not only to pay careful attention to them, but also to recognize the factors that give them influence on decisions—or undermine that influence. The gap between stated goals and the goals actually pursued is sometimes surprisingly wide. Recognizing when there is a gap and being aware of the factors that influence it are particularly valuable for a system outsider, who may otherwise be easily misled by formal goal statements. This chapter examines goals—both stated and unstated.

A. STATED GOALS

Discussions of competition law often pay much attention to stated goals because we generally assume that they guide decisions. If a Competition Authority (CA) says the law's goal is to protect consumers from excessive price increases, this goal probably will be a factor in its decisions. But it is important to look carefully at what the CA actually does before we rely on this claim. Often this information can be gathered from the internet and other published sources, but in many systems those with significant recent experience of the CA's activities are even more valuable. Stated goals usually guide an institution's decisions if (1) the institution is well protected from outside influences, (2) competition law itself is developed to the point where a path to the goals is widely recognized and accepted, (3) the decision-makers are personally committed to pursuing the goals, and (4) the institution has sufficient political and financial support to pursue them.

Competition Law and Antitrust. David J. Gerber, Oxford University Press (2020). © David J. Gerber.
DOI: 10.1093/oso/9780198727477.001.0001

To the extent that these conditions are not met the goals are less likely to be dependable.

Goals are important not only for predicting future decisions, but also for another and less obvious reason—they tell us what arguments and claims are acceptable and likely to be effective. The goals justify arguments that are consistent with them and invalidate those that are not. If, for example, the stated goal of competition law is the welfare of consumers, a lawyer is not likely to be successful if she argues to a competition law official that a particular outcome will advance the cause of democracy.

It is often useful to view goal statements as messages, because this points to potentially relevant questions. "Who sent the message? Who were the intended recipients? How much influence is it likely to have on specific types of decision-makers?" Answers to these questions can be especially valuable for a system outsider, because they focus on how the stated goals are actually used. Insiders may be familiar with these factors, but outsiders may not recognize them. Legislatures, courts, and CAs all send goal messages.

Legislatures sometimes state goals. Formally, the messages in statutes are addressed to *domestic institutions*. They tell administrative officials and courts what they should do. They may also be directed at *domestic constituencies*. For example, they may be intended to satisfy wealthy potential supporters ("Hey, big spender, look what I am doing for you.") or powerful political groups.

Messages may also be designed to appeal to *foreign institutions or firms*. They may be used to "advertise" a country's relationship to the market and/or to the "rule of law," particularly where there has been a recent change of government. For example, an emerging market government may use goal statements to signal its willingness to support free markets, hoping thereby to attract foreign investment or to acquire loans or other support from foreign lending institutions. In these contexts a goal statement may be best seen primarily as a form of marketing that may not reflect what decision-makers actually do.

Courts in most competition law regimes have little or no authority to articulate goals and seldom do so, but in some they are highly influential in setting goals that decision-makers generally follow. In the US, for example, the courts are the most authoritative source of goal statements. In particular, US Supreme Court opinions provide the primary goal guidance for courts as well as administrative agencies.

CAs also make claims about goals. They seldom have "binding effect," but the CA is typically the primary enforcer, so what it says about what it will do is often a valuable guide to what it actually will do. Experienced practitioners often pay careful attention to those claims.

We can now look at the goals themselves. In some systems, the stated goals are solely "economic," while in others they also include the social and political impact of competition law.

B. ECONOMIC GOALS

The "competition" in "competition law" refers to economic competition, so in that general sense competition law goals always relate to this competition. That is important, but it does not tell us very much about the variety of goals that competition law regimes pursue. Before looking at these goals we need to clarify some basic aspects of economic competition. Economists and experienced competition law people can skip this basic material, but for most others it will be valuable or even necessary for understanding competition law issues.[1]

Competition occurs on a market of some kind, which is essentially a space of encounter and exchange between those who offer to supply a good or service and those who might wish to purchase it. Markets can be physical (the local food market) or digital (the internet). In a market the suppliers have incentives to make their offers as attractive to buyers as possible—for example, by selling at a lower price than their competitors or providing a better product. Each buyer has incentives to pay the lowest available price for the product she wants.

---

[1] There are, of course, many books and other works that further explain the functioning of markets. For a succinct and accessible treatment that is also related to competition law issues, see Ernest Gellhorn, William Kovacic, and Stephen Calkins, *Competition Law and Economics* (5th ed., 2004). For deeper, but still accessible treatments of the economics of markets and competition, see Massimo Motta, *Competition Policy* (2004) and Keith N. Hylton, *Antitrust Law: Economic Theory and Common Law Evolution* (2003).

Where there is no coercion or other interference with this exchange, both sides freely enter into an arrangement which they consider beneficial. For example, the vegetable seller sells her vegetables at the best price she can reasonably expect to get and the buyer buys her vegetables at the lowest price she can expect to pay. Both the vegetable seller and the vegetable buyer are satisfied—perhaps even happy. From a broader perspective, the market is directing resources to those uses that the society as a whole most wants fulfilled (economists refer to this as the society's "highest and best uses"). Note, however, that what "society" refers to is not always clear, particularly in global markets. Note also that those with the most resources in the society (however defined) have the greatest potential influence on what the market provides.

Any interference with this free operation of demand and supply reduces the benefits to both participants and society. If, for example, the government restricts the prices at which vegetables can be sold on the market, sellers will no longer be satisfied. Buyers may be happier for a time because they can buy at a lower price, but they may not be happy for long. The price controls are likely to lead producers to invest fewer or no resources in producing vegetables. This not only reduces the satisfaction of the buyers, but it also means that the society gets less of a product than it would have been willing to pay for it. Private actors can intentionally distort the market for their own benefit. For example, where the producers of the vegetables agree with each other to raise prices, they benefit from the higher prices, at least for a time, but buyers are harmed. The society pays more to produce the same amount of vegetables. Moreover, buyers are likely to react by buying fewer vegetables and therefore not satisfying their desire for vegetables. Competition law combats these harmful distortions, because they reduce the economic benefits that markets can provide.

Economic goals fall into three basic groups: system-function goals, outcome goals, and economic freedom goals.

1. SYSTEM-FUNCTION GOALS

These goals focus on maintaining or improving how the economic system functions.

a. Market structure

One way to improve system function is to improve its structure. The basic idea is that a market's "structure" determines the way it functions because it shapes the participants' incentives to compete. Accordingly, improving market structure improves the way the system functions. "Structure" here basically refers to the relative market shares of the competitors. Consider three different structures: (1) one firm in the market (a monopolist) has no competitors, so its only incentive to reduce prices or improve product may be to prevent new firms from entering the market; (2) five firms in the market, but one has 80 percent market share and the others each have only 5 percent—the smaller competitors have incentives to compete or to leave the market, but the market leader already has control of the market, so its incentives to compete may be limited; and (3) three competitors have similar market shares—all have strong incentives to compete against each other. In each case, the structure of the market shapes competition.

Competition law should, therefore, try to deter conduct that impairs market structure. For example, a merger between the two leading competitors on a market will change the market structure, increase the economic power of the merged firm, and reduce the incentives for others to compete in the market. As a result, it is likely to harm competition and should be prevented—unless it can be justified in some other way. This view of competition (often referred to as the structure-conduct-performance or SCP model) was prominent among economists during the decades after the Second World War.

These so-called "Harvard School" views penetrated US antitrust law during the 1950s and 1960s and soon spread to Germany and then to the EU. Some systems continue to rely on market structure analysis, in part because it is relatively easy to understand and apply without extensive training in economics.

b. Economic efficiency

Many economists grew dissatisfied with market structure analysis as the core of competition law. They generally accept that market structure influences competition, but they view it as too blunt an instrument to be used reliably to support competition law decisions. They argue that harm to competition should be determined by reference to the dynamics of markets—*how they function*—rather than to their structure. This view focuses on the "*efficiency*" of markets and their capacity to direct resources to their "highest and best" uses. It provides a more scientific and precise way of identifying and measuring the *effects* of specific conduct under specific circumstances, and thus it avoids broad structure-based approaches that may condemn conduct that is harmful under some circumstances, but not others. This approach also allows CAs and judges to defend their decisions in more rigorous and consistent ways.

The central criterion for assessing competitive harm in this view is whether conduct has raised (or will raise) the market price above a competitive price. An artificially created price increase distorts market signals and directs resources away from their most valued uses. This view (often associated with the "Chicago School" of economics) became prominent in US antitrust beginning in the 1970s, where it soon came to dominate competition law thinking. Since the 1990s it has become increasingly influential in Europe and, more recently, elsewhere. As we shall see later (Ch. 12) concerns about the power of "Big Data" (Amazon, Google, etc.) have challenged its value in some areas of competition law.

c. Consumer welfare

The broader, but related idea of "consumer welfare" has become increasingly popular in many competition laws. It is easier to understand and more politically appealing than references to economic efficiency. Its most basic functions are to exclude political and social goals from competition law consideration and to make clear that effects on producers are not to be considered in the analysis for most purposes. It is closely related to efficiency goals, because the core idea is that greater efficiency benefits consumers by forcing prices toward the lowest sustainable level. The concept can also include, however, other types of consumer harm. The label is politically attractive, because virtually everyone is a consumer.

Note that the term "consumer welfare" is used in different ways, so it is important to identify who is using it and how. For economists it has the technical meaning mentioned above, but non-economists often use the term in a broader sense, referring merely to some unspecified benefit for consumers.

System-function goals share a potentially very valuable characteristic: *The path to the goal can be identified with some precision.* Economists have studied the conditions under which particular conduct can create harm, and they have developed methods that can be used to assess whether conduct has had a harmful effect. Moreover, science requires that the basis for making that assessment be stated, so that others can evaluate whether the method is sound and being properly used. In addition, these methods use quantifiable criteria, which makes the effects of the conduct measurable. Competition law can use these methods to determine whether and to what extent conduct has particular harmful effects. This identifies the path to the goal and requires that decisions be justifiable in accordance with the methods.

An example may be useful. Assume that three firms (A, B, C) each have 20 percent of the market for a particular mineral used in producing LED screens. They agree with each other to restrict their combined output of the product by 5 percent in the belief that this reduction in supply will increase the market price of the mineral and increase their profits. Economic science can evaluate with some precision whether this conduct will cause the desired increase in price above the competitive price and thereby harm buyers of the product and distort the functioning of the market. The methods a CA uses to make this assessment are known, and others can criticize a CA's decision for failure to follow them appropriately. This contrasts sharply with the outcome goals discussed below where the path from particular conduct to the outcome may be murky and unclear.

System-function goals predominate in more developed and wealthier regimes, and they have become increasingly attractive in many other regimes as well. Why? First, they are narrow and often based on solid economic reasoning, which makes decisions based on them easier to defend both legally and politically. Second, in promising to improve the way the market functions they offer benefits to all who are affected by the market and, as a result, they have a broad base of potential support.

2. OUTCOME GOALS

Goals often refer to outcomes that competition law is expected to produce—for example, lower prices, more economic development, or less economic inequality—rather than protection of competition itself. The way the system functions influences the outcomes it produces of course, but focusing on outcomes changes the way we view competition law. As noted above, a focus on outcomes cannot clearly identify the path to competition law decisions, because many factors contribute to any economic outcome. As a result, it gives a decision-maker discretion to decide which factor or factors are relevant to the goal. This reduces predictability and tends to undermine claims that enforcement is based on legal rather than political or other factors.

Outcome goals are attractive to decision-makers for several reasons. First, they are easy to understand. For example, everyone knows what it means to reduce prices. Second, they often appeal to widespread popular concerns—such as price levels. Third, they are usually broad and general, allowing them to be used in a variety of political contexts. And fourth, they can be applied by officials and judges with limited training in competition law or economics. Reducing prices is a particularly popular outcome goal (as consumers we all want lower prices)! If a government claims that competition law can reduce prices, it is more likely to attract political support than if it promises greater efficiency—an abstract idea that many will not understand or care much about.

In developed and politically well-supported competition law regimes, especially functioning democracies, outcome goals tend to be less prominent for two main reasons. One is obvious: an established competition law regime typically has less need to seek popular support than a newer, less established regime. The other may be less obvious. Such regimes often have stronger incentives to apply the law consistently and to justify their decisions on a rationally defensible basis than regimes in more authoritarian or politically unstable contexts.

The goal of reducing prices illustrates some of these issues. How does a decision-maker decide which of the many factors that influence prices are the result of restraints of competition. Some factors are natural—for example, crop disasters; others are political (interference by a government) or social (food riots). Any change in supply or demand on a market can lead to price changes. This makes it difficult or impossible to establish which factors have led to the increase. How can competition law confidently identify when particular conduct rather than some other factor "causes" an increase in prices? Without a firm basis for identifying conduct as harmful, competition law decision-makers face much uncertainty, and this can easily increase the risk for corruption.

Another disadvantage of using price reduction as a competition law goal is that it tends to blur the distinction between competition law and price controls. It is common to hear officials in some regimes (particularly newer ones) say that they applied competition law to reduce prices when, on closer examination, it turns out that they simply demanded price reductions. This is bureaucratic price control, not competition law. The core idea of competition law is that it combats restraints on competition, while price control regimes can merely order a reduction in price. This distinction can be difficult to recognize, particularly in competition law regimes that are new, but it is fundamental. Note that competition law officials have often been recruited from price control offices (e.g., China after 2008).

3. ECONOMIC FREEDOM

The goal of economic freedom links the political and emotional appeal of freedom as a value to the claim that economic freedom is the essence of competition—that is, that competition requires economic liberty if it is to function at all. These ideas have been highly influential at times, and in some regimes they are still influential. They were prominent in the US during several periods prior to the "revolution" of the 1970s, and they have also been influential in the evolution of competition law in Europe. In both contexts, the goal of economic freedom has been nourished by deep cultural roots and attachment to freedom as an independent value. The goal is, however, difficult to apply as an independent basis for competition law decisions. Questions such as "how much freedom?" and "freedom from what?" create much uncertainty. Nevertheless, in some contexts the goal functions as a politically attractive support for competition law.

C. SOCIAL AND POLITICAL GOALS

Some goals are social or political rather than economic. Most competition law regimes have featured goals such as fairness, equality of opportunity, and support for democracy at some point or points in their evolution. Prior to the 1970s US antitrust law often emphasized them. In Europe, they have also often been prominent, particularly in the context of the German social market economy. They are a focus of many newer competition law regimes and in emerging markets, where competition law is not well known or widely accepted, because they attract political support, require relatively few resources, and can be applied without extensive knowledge of economics.

1. FAIRNESS: THE GOAL OF FAIRNESS HAS PARTICULARLY BROAD POLITICAL APPEAL

Fairness takes two quite different forms. *Competitive fairness* refers to relations among competitors. If, for example, one firm has advantages over others because it is politically connected or uses its size to coerce buyers not to buy from its competitors, its conduct is likely to be considered unfair. The promise of competitive fairness attracts support among those who fear and/or envy powerful firms, especially foreign firms. It is often associated with other social and political goals such as the goal of increasing economic opportunity for small and medium-sized firms. *Consumer fairness* is fundamentally different. It protects consumers from harm inflicted by economically powerful firms, particularly where they use their power to extract high prices from consumers. The goal is politically attractive, especially in low income countries and countries in which market prices are volatile or controlled by foreign interests.

2. DISPERSING POWER: THE LEVEL PLAYING FIELD

The goals of dispersing economic power and improving economic opportunities for smaller firms are often combined. Where markets are dominated by large firms and minimal competition, income inequality tends to increase, social mobility tends to decrease, and democracy may be threatened. For some, competition law can and should be used, therefore, to disperse power and counteract these tendencies. Such concerns were central to the enactment of US antitrust law in 1890 and remained significant at times until the 1970s. They continue to be a factor in some contexts in Europe, where they are sometimes linked to concern that inequality threatens the process of European integration. They tend to be prominent among Latin American regimes in which concern for social justice has strong political support. Nevertheless, their focus on society-wide effects makes them difficult to apply to specific conduct in a consistent way.

Economic and non-economic goals can mix in many ways, and identifying the strands of influence often illuminates decisions, discussions, and claims. Non-economic goals tend to diminish in importance in favor of economic goals where a competition law regime becomes better established and thus better able to articulate the benefits it offers. Nevertheless, they continue to have value in attracting political support, and they seldom disappear permanently and completely from any system.

D. UNSTATED GOALS

In many competition law regimes, particularly in emerging market countries and authoritarian states, it is common for institutions and individuals to pursue goals that are not stated or even acknowledged. Their impact is often difficult to evaluate, particularly by an outsider to the system, but being aware of them and of the incentives that engender them can be very valuable. We will return to these influences in the next chapter, but I mention them here to emphasize their relation to stated goals. They are seldom mentioned in writing about competition law, but they are often well known to insiders.

Corruption—payment to officials in order to influence their decisions—is especially harmful. It is a scourge on competition law in many countries, undermining the commitment of officials to use competition law effectively and impairing public confidence in their efforts. It is most common where officials are poorly paid, and these are the same countries in which there is much skepticism about competition law. Recognizing the factors that encourage corruption can alert an outsider to the need to investigate its existence and extent (see Ch. 4).

Sometimes governments themselves impose unstated goals. Where, for example, a government's general policy is to protect its high-tech firms from competition, it may use competition law to further that goal. It will seldom admit that it is using competition law for such protectionist purposes, but looking at patterns in recent competition law decisions often reveals this influence. This provides a sounder basis for assessing decisions than relying solely on the language of formal goals. It also helps to identify the kinds of lawyers and advisers that are likely to be useful sources of information and support.

The global arena itself induces decision-makers to pursue unstated goals. For example, CAs and officials have incentives to seek status within global competition law networks. This often leads officials to align their decisions and/or claims with the wealthier and more powerful members of the network. This can provide them with resources and influence, and it increases the likelihood that their proposals and requests will be accepted by other CAs. It may also increase a CA's leverage in acquiring resources and support from its home government.

Finally, ideologies create unstated goals. Decisions that reflect or support a particular ideology signal membership within a group and can generate support from others who share the ideology. Ideologies can influence individual officials, but they can also influence a CA or an entire bureaucracy.

The goals of competition law shape not only competition law decisions, but also the way decisions are discussed and justified. In this chapter we have noted the main goals and indicated some of the ways governments use them. In the following chapter we look at the paths from goals to decisions.

4

INSTITUTIONS AND METHODS: IMPLEMENTING COMPETITION LAW GOALS

Institutions, procedures, and methods shape the paths from goals to decisions. Much happens along the way. In this chapter, we examine that path. Who makes the decisions? What are their incentives and influences? Which methods do they use for which purposes? The focus is on decisions both formal and informal and on the influences that shape them.

A tension is ever present: the goals of competition law often clash with powerful economic and political interests, and the clash occurs in institutions. Competition law constrains business firms in their pursuit of profits, and when it does they try to avoid or combat it. This conflict lurks behind all competition law decisions.

A. LEGISLATURES: ROLES AND INFLUENCES

Competition law has to be created! It does not emerge "naturally." Modern societies need property and contract law (there have to be some rules!) so these laws emerge naturally through custom and agreement, and all societies have them. In contrast, the government must create competition law—by legislating it into existence or in some other way authorizing domestic institutions to take action against anticompetitive conduct. Often it becomes an isolated piece of legislation, giving decision-makers limited sources of guidance for interpreting and applying the law. As a result, many have little choice but to turn to foreign sources for guidance.

Competition Law and Antitrust. David J. Gerber, Oxford University Press (2020). © David J. Gerber.
DOI: 10.1093/oso/9780198727477.001.0001

1. ACTION MESSAGES

It is often useful to see the legislature's rules and principles as "action messages" (as distinct from the "goal messages" we noted in the previous chapter). This directs us to two important questions: where is the legislature directing the messages? And why? This again provides a strategy for penetrating complexity and seeing more by focusing on less.

To domestic institutions: Formally, a competition statute is directed to domestic institutions. It authorizes them to act in specified ways in response to specified forms of conduct, and it typically also provides penalties for violating the law. It may do little more than authorize governmental intervention in a vaguely defined category of conduct. For example, the main conduct rules of US antitrust law are based on two very general provisions of an 1890 statute (the Sherman Act). Section 1 prohibits agreements that constitute a "restraint of trade"; section 2 prohibits "monopolization." As we will see later (Ch. 8) there are a few additional provisions in a later statute but interpretation of these two extremely simple provisions of the Sherman Act has yielded most of the substantive US antitrust law.[1] In contrast, most other competition laws are far more detailed, often describing in detail what kind of conduct is subject to which penalties.

A statute's influence on the decisions of institutions depends on many factors that we will soon discuss, including the institution's independence from political and economic influences, its resources, and the political context in which it operates.

To businesses: The messages are also addressed to businesses that may violate the statute: "If you do X, this is what can happen to you." The primary addressees are typically domestic firms, but in a globalized economy the addressees often include foreign firms. For example, when China's competition law was enacted in 2007 the government apparently saw it as a message to foreign firms that Chinese markets would now be subject to

---

[1] Sherman Antitrust Act, ch. 647, 26 Stat. 209 (codified as amended at 15 USC §§ 1–7) (2018).

rules similar to those of other major markets and therefore safe for their investments.[2]

To domestic stakeholders: Legislatures can use competition laws to attract support from voters and powerful economic and political interests.

To foreign institutions: Finally, competition legislation is sometimes intended to demonstrate to transnational institutions and foreign governments that a government is committed to free markets and the rule of law.

2. STATUTORY FEATURES: CLUES TO COMPETITION LAW DYNAMICS

Competition law statutes vary widely in length, structure, and tone, and these characteristics often provide valuable insights into how the domestic system functions. We can sometimes learn a lot about a statute's role simply by knowing what to look for in these characteristics.

A statute's length and language are often revealing. Some are brief and simple, giving enforcement institutions extensive discretion in applying them. This increases the status of institutions that exercise this discretion. For example, as we have seen, the basic US antitrust statute is exceptionally brief and general (see Ch. 8). This puts the federal courts at the center of the antitrust system, because they have the authority to make final (and binding) decisions about the statute's meaning. Where statutes are more detailed and specific, institutions that interpret and apply them have less discretion and generally less power.

Structure can provide similar clues. Some statutes are highly systematic—that is, the pieces fit neatly together.[3] This requires that claims and arguments be presented and articulated within that systematic structure and language. A less systematic statute allows a greater range of claims and arguments.

---

[2] Anti-Monopoly Law of the People's Republic of China (promulgated by the Standing Comm. Nat'l People's Cong., August 30, 2007, effective August 1, 2008) CLI.1.96789 (EN) (Lawinfochina).

[3] Federal Republic of Germany, Act Against Restraints on Competition ch. 1–2, as amended by Article 10(9) of the Act of October 30, 2017, BUNDESKARTELLAMT.

3. COMPLIANCE

The remedies a statute provides are often central to its influence on conduct. Some statutes merely provide a Competition Authority (CA) with authority to intervene in business decision-making, while others provide high fines for specific types of violations. Knowing the remedies available in specific situations and identifying who can and does impose them can be of great value.

The most common remedies are:

a. Contract invalidity

Statutes often declare contracts that violate their provisions invalid and unenforceable. Contracts are the basis of most competition law violations, so knowing that a contract may be unenforceable is likely to reduce its value to participants. For example, cartel agreements are typically less attractive if they cannot be enforced against individual cartel members.

b. Fines

Most statutes provide that a CA or a court may impose fines for violations under certain circumstances, and they usually specify the amount of the fines that may be imposed.

c. Administrative intervention

Some statutes merely authorize a CA to acquire information about potential violations and/or to negotiate with violators to eliminate the conduct.

d. Private enforcement

Finally, a legislature may enable private parties to seek compensation from violators for harm caused by the violation. In some systems, this remedy can be pursued only after the CA has acted, whereas in others a private litigant may go to court without prior administrative action. We will look at this more closely later.

4. CHANGING THE LEGISLATION

The frequency and extent of legislative changes may also provide clues to a regime's dynamics. Some legislatures play an active role in competition law by frequently revising the relevant legislation. This typically leads to closer coordination with the enforcement agency and often greater influence, but it also invites more attention from lobbyists. Other legislatures rarely change the statute and play a less central role in the system.

5. THE LEGISLATURE AS A DIRECT INFLUENCE ON ENFORCEMENT

A legislature may influence enforcement by influencing the CA. Legislatures often control a CA's budget, and individual legislators sometimes use this control to "discourage" a CA from enforcing competition law against a firm that has secured the legislator's "protection": "If you block that merger, you can expect cuts in your budget next year." The legislature may also be in a position to influence appointments to a CA.

These factors underscore the need to look carefully at the roles that legislatures play in a competition law regime.

B. COMPETITION AUTHORITIES

CAs are charged with implementing competition law goals. They play central roles in all competition law regimes, primarily because they make most, sometimes all, significant enforcement decisions. Understanding a regime's CA is often at least as important as knowing the formal law—often far more important.

1. ROLES

CAs play many roles, and there are major differences among regimes in how they view and perform their roles. This often leads to misunderstandings and false expectations in dealing with them. A lawyer familiar with one CA often assumes that other CAs function more or less the same way. This is can be a dangerous assumption!

Each CA has its own culture—a shared set of attitudes, priorities, and values about the role of the institution and the conduct of its members. Some CAs, for example, focus on how "tough" they are in enforcing the competition statute, whereas others focus on educating the business community about competition law or negotiating with business leaders to change their behavior. This is particularly common in newer competition law regimes that have uncertain political backing.

a. The operating code

A CA adds content, definition, and detail to the formal law, sometimes sharing that role with courts, but often playing the central role. Its decisions and pronouncements represent an operating code that practitioners and their clients look to in making business decisions. Larger, better funded CAs such as the EU competition directorate often provide numerous regulations and guidelines that give guidance to firms and their lawyers. Typically they also provide extensive and accessible information about their past activities. Smaller and newer CAs are less likely to publish such guidelines, and they often do not provide detailed records of their past practices and decisions. This makes it more difficult for outsiders to know what to expect, and it enhances the value of "insider" contacts for those concerned about violating the law.

b. Gathering market data

In order to implement goals effectively, a CA ideally gathers, organizes, and analyzes data about market conditions and price patterns. This is especially true in the early stages of competition law development, when a CA may have limited knowledge of market conditions. For example, COMESA (the Common Market for East and South Africa) began competition law operations in 2015, and it has often underscored the importance of data-gathering.[4] Even in developed systems such as the EU, however, it continues to be a focus of compliance efforts. The need for abundant and accurate data is particularly prominent where a regime relies on economic analysis in evaluating conduct. Sophisticated data-gathering and analysis is, however, expensive, and less well-funded CAs are often unable to afford it.

---

[4] COMESA, 'Statistics' (*COMESA*) < https://www.comesa.int/statistics-unit/ > accessed October 14, 2019.

c. Educating businesses

A firm cannot be expected to comply with competition law un-less its decision-makers know about the provisions and what they mean, so many CAs pay much attention to educating firms about competition law. These efforts have been central in the evolution of competition law in Europe, and they are still a focus of activity in many emerging markets. Other regimes (e.g., US) tend to as-sume that firms are at least aware of the basic content of competi-tion law and pay less attention to educating them about it.

d. Cooperation and negotiation

Dialogue and negotiation tend to be less expensive than formal pursuit and litigation for increasing compliance, so these tools are especially attractive to smaller and less well-funded CAs.

e. Advocacy within government

Promoting competition within the government itself is an im-portant task for many CAs. Some have the right to comment on, delay, or even block decisions by other agencies that might harm competition. In Italy, for example, the drafters of the first compe-tition law statute (enacted in 1990) included a provision that gives the CA the right to comment on governmental measures that might harm competition and requires agencies considering such action to consult with the CA before taking certain potentially harmful measures.[5] China created similar requirements in 2017.[6]

f. Enforcement

Enforcement through litigation and formal sanctions is the most expensive means of promoting compliance, but it is sometimes necessary to use them to deter harmful conduct. In the US and Europe, it is now often the central task of CAs, while in newer CAs it tends to play a more minor role.

---

[5] Law No. 287/1990 of October 10, 1990 (*Norme per la tutela della concorrenza e del mercato*).

[6] [Anti-Unfair Competition Law] (promulgated by the Standing Comm. of the Nat'l People's Cong. of the People's Republic of China, amended November 4, 2017, effective January 1, 2018).

Enforcement requires evidence of a potential violation. CAs often possess and use investigation tools that include demands for the production of data as well as testimony of company officials. Some also have authority to engage in so-called "dawn raids." Imagine a situation in which officials from the CA appear without warning at your headquarters at the start of business one day and demand access to your data—including computers and other files. This is a much feared "dawn raid." In some systems a court must authorize such dawn raids, but the element of surprise is critical to the success of a dawn raid, so court authorizations tend to be quick and sometimes of limited scope. Officials may then walk away from your offices with your computers and files, and there may be little you can do to protect against this.

Enforcement proceedings vary significantly in the extent to which defendants can participate and contest the CA's findings. Developed competition law systems typically provide significant rights of participation and defense, but newer systems often do not. Moreover, the procedural rights of the defendant companies vary significantly.

A CA typically has three main enforcement tools. One is to impose a fine on a company that it finds to be violating the competition law. The authority to impose fines is often a CA's main tool. These fines can be very high.[7] Another is to prohibit specified conduct that it considers to be a violation. For example, this is its primary tool for combating harmful mergers (see Ch. 7). Less common, but much feared, is its authority to impose or recommend criminal sanctions on individuals responsible for the harmful conduct. These are cases in which the conduct was

---

[7] <https://www.jftc.go.jp/en/pressreleases/yearly-2019/September/190926. pdf> Office of Public Affairs, 'StarKist Ordered to Pay $100 Million Criminal Fine for Antitrust Violation' (*Dep't of Justice*, September 11, 2019) <https://www.justice. gov/opa/pr/starkist-ordered-pay-100-million-criminal-fine-antitrust-violation> accessed October 7, 2019; European Commission, 'Commission Fines Google €1.49 Billion for Abusive Practices in Online Advertising' (*European Commission*, March 20, 2019) <https://europa.eu/rapid/press-release_IP-19-1770_en.htm> accessed October 7, 2019; Japan Fair Trade Commission, 'The JFTC Issued Cease and Desist Orders and Surcharge Payment Orders to Manufacturers of Aluminum Beverage Cans and Steel Beverage Cans' (*Japan Fair Trade Commission*, September 26, 2019) <https://www.jftc.go.jp/en/pressreleases/yearly-2019/September/190926.pdf> accessed October 7, 2019.

clearly a violation—predominantly cases of agreements among competitors to restrain trade, so the law considers personal sanctions appropriate as a means of deterring knowing violation of its provisions. Criminal sanctions were rare outside the US until recently, but these have grown significantly in number and severity in both the US and several other countries. Most CAs cannot themselves bring criminal charges, but if criminal liability is available, the CA must refer appropriate cases to the criminal courts for prosecution.

A CA's enforcement actions are often subject to review by courts, but, as we shall see later in this chapter, there are different types of review, and different types of courts perform the reviews.

2. CAPACITIES, CAPABILITIES, AND RESOURCES

Size, capabilities, and resources are major factors in determining which of these functions a CA performs and how it performs them.

a. Resources

Resources are critical. If a CA has limited resources, it must rely on low cost enforcement strategies such as education and negotiation, and it probably cannot engage in the kind of sophisticated economic analysis that a large and well-funded CA performs. This is especially significant where a CA may be required to defend its decisions in court, where it may be opposed by highly trained and experienced lawyers and economists hired by wealthy opponents. This tends to discourage a CA from applying the law to such firms.

b. Size, capabilities, and structure

CAs vary greatly in size. Some are large, employing hundreds of professionals, including lawyers, economists, and computer specialists, but most are much smaller—some with only a few employees. This also influences what a CA can do and how it can perform the tasks it wishes to perform.

The capabilities of a CA's employees are particularly important in this context. The education, experience, and knowledge level of employees shape what a CA can do, but attracting and maintaining highly qualified and experienced officials requires adequate funds. Large legal and economic firms can usually pay far more for talent than a CA can pay. As a result, officials in many CAs are often young and inexperienced, and they often have less technological and analytical capability than the firms that oppose them.

Recognizing a CA's structure—that is, the distribution of power and authority within the institution—is important in predicting its decisions. For example, in some CAs the president (or other top official) has extensive control over all decisions, while in others s/he may be prohibited by law or custom from intervening or even participating in many decisions (e.g., in Germany, individual "decision units" make decisions about cases independently of the president). Structure can be a particularly important predictor of the role of economics. In some CAs (e.g., the EU) economists are integrated into case evaluation from early in the process, whereas in others (e.g., Japan) economists are less routinely integrated in actual case decision-making. The extent of integration influences how economic and legal methods are combined in decision making.

3. INSTITUTIONAL INDEPENDENCE

Where a CA can act relatively independently—that is, take decisions primarily on the basis of established principles and methods, its decisions are likely to be relatively predictable. Often, however, external pressures and incentives reduce this independence, so examining these factors can reveal much about what the CA can and will do.

a. Political pressures

A CA is usually part of the administrative branch of government, where it will be vulnerable to pressures from other parts of the government. For example, if the Ministry of Commerce emphasizes harm caused by foreign dominant firms, it may use its status or position to pressure the CA to take action against such firms. A CA that is subject to influence from other governmental institutions generally operates very differently from one that is free of such pressures.

b. Economic incentives

Financial incentives can also influence decisions. These may take the form of payments to officials for favorable decisions, but they may also be more subtle and indirect. For example, a private lawyer or economist in a CA who expects to enter or re-enter private practice is aware that her decisions as a competition official may affect her prospects in private practice. S/he may or may not be influenced by this awareness.

4. PASSIONS

The personal commitment of officials to the CA's goals is often a powerful influence on competition law decisions. For example, the successes of the German CA (FCO), especially during its early decades (ca. 1960–1990) owe much to the commitment of officials who often shared a fervent conviction that competition law could help to create a new kind of society in Germany. Similarly, competition officials in the European Commission have often been motivated by the conviction that competition law would help create a better Europe. In Africa, the personal commitment of officials such as George Lipimile in Zambia and then in COMESA have been a major factor in the successes of CAs there. Without such commitment, obstacles in the path of competition law are difficult to overcome.

C. COURTS

Courts play a range of roles in competition law regimes. In some regimes (e.g., US) their role is central, while in others it is marginal. Assumptions about what courts can and cannot do can be highly misleading and lead to costly errors! Those outside a system often misunderstand the roles of foreign courts—until it is too late.

1. ROLES

Review of administrative decisions: Courts typically have authority to review CA decisions, but the critical issues are "Which courts?",

"What can they review?", and "When?" In many regimes, courts can only review a CA's decision for procedural error or constitutional violations such as bias or duress. In some, however, courts are also authorized and/or required to review CA decisions for errors in interpreting or applying the substantive law. This allows courts to shape the content of competition law, so it is extremely important to be aware of whether courts can do this and under what circumstances. The more important the role of a court, the greater its exposure to external pressures (including corruption). Many officials (especially from emerging market regimes) complain that reviewing courts are often influenced by such pressures.

Private enforcement: Private enforcement gives courts additional roles. It is necessary to distinguish between two varieties of private enforcement. In the "pure" version, a firm or individual may go directly to court to claim a remedy for harm from anticompetitive conduct. It need not wait for a public enforcement agency to take action. This version has been central to the US antitrust regime almost since its inception (see Ch. 7) but elsewhere it has been made available much more recently, if at all, and it typically plays a more limited role.

More common is the follow-on or "piggyback" version, where private litigation follows administrative action—either because this is legally required or because it is practically necessary. Some regimes require that a CA act first before a private plaintiff is permitted to bring a law suit. This reflects a reluctance to burden courts with the fact-finding called for in competition law cases. Even where such actions are authorized, however, obstacles to acquiring evidence make them rare (e.g., Japan). Procedural systems typically do not allow a plaintiff to demand information from a defendant or others except perhaps where they can demonstrate to a judge that specific information is *directly relevant to an element of the claimed violation*. As a result, a plaintiff must wait for a CA to acquire more extensive data that it may then use to pursue litigation.

2. COURT TYPES AND STRUCTURES

It is important to be clear about what a court can and cannot do, and what its obligations and tools are.

Administrative courts: Administrative courts can typically review CA decisions only on procedural or sometimes also nonconstitutional safeguards. They seldom have authority to review CA decisions on substantive grounds.

General jurisdiction courts: can sometimes review CA decisions on substantive grounds, but judges that deal with many different kinds of cases are not likely to be comfortable with the fact-dense, economics-based requirements of competition law. As a result, they are often reluctant to deal with substantive issues, preferring to settle cases on procedural issues. Some regimes have created specialized "chambers" within courts to review competition law cases.

Specialized courts and tribunals: Some channel administrative appeals to specialized tribunals. These institutions may be integrated into the judicial system and led by regular judges or they may be outside it, in which case the judges often include politicians and representatives of businesses and labor unions. In all cases, it can be particularly valuable to know who the judges are and how they are chosen.

3. CAPACITIES AND INCENTIVES

Court structures can also provide valuable insights into the way competition law works. In some (mainly common law) systems judges are often appointed late in their careers and do not normally expect "promotion" to a higher court. This allows them to take decisions with limited concern for personal advancement. In most systems, however, a judge becomes part of a hierarchy after her university training and remains in that hierarchy for her entire career. Her salary and status depend on her position in it, so s/he is likely to hesitate to make decisions that are not in line with the decisions of the judges that will influence her career. Moreover, the complexity and uncertainty of competition law pose significant risks for error and unclear reasoning, and the economic importance of many cases can make them politically sensitive. These can be powerful incentives for courts to resolve competition law matters on procedural rather than substantive grounds.

D. HOW THEY DECIDE: METHODS

Methods (formal or informal; recognized or implicit) shape decisions. Identifying the methods used provides a valuable tool for interpreting past decisions, predicting future decisions, and influencing decision-makers. It allows us to view issues the same way the decision-maker does, and this makes it more likely that we can predict what s/he might do or even influence her. Courts and CAs typically use both legal and economic methods, but they mix them differently. Judges tend to rely on traditional legal methods while many CAs rely more heavily on economic methods (especially where economists hold leadership positions).

Traditional legal methods *focus on language* in making decisions. They focus on written texts such as statutes, case opinions, and regulations. These texts *describe* violations, and the decision-maker makes decisions by placing the conduct at issue within the categories described in the text or creating others that s/he considers authorized by the text.

In contrast, economic methods focus on *numbers*. They identify patterns and causal relationships within available data sets. In many regimes, the central question is whether conduct had or is likely to have particular kinds of economic effects—for example, whether an agreement was responsible for a price increase or a merger can be expected to reduce the competitiveness of a market, and economics is the most potentially valuable tool for doing this.

In practice, the two methods are interwoven. The training, professional position, and incentives of the decision-maker determine which strands are most influential in a specific context. The greater the role and status of economists in the decision-making process, the greater the influence of economic methods is likely to be, and the same is true with regard to law trained officials.

1. INTERPRETING STATUTES

How a statute is interpreted depends on the type of reasoning used in the relevant legal system. Judges and lawyers are trained in particular methods of interpretation. Some methods (e.g., Germany and Japan) are finely honed, systematic, and seriously studied. Grasping basic principles of these methods in a particular legal system can help an outsider to assess decisions and to communicate more effectively with those trained in those methods. Even a few hours of reading or discussing the methods with a regime insider can be very valuable. In other systems, however, methods are less well developed, which makes it more difficult to interpret and predict decisions. Where a CA's decisions are subject to substantive judicial review, it has strong incentives to adhere closely to the interpretive methods of courts. Otherwise, it may not.

2. USING PRIOR CASES

Institutions use prior cases to provide authority for their decisions and to increase consistency in the outcomes produced. Courts must pay much attention to authority issues—for example, which courts have stated which legal principles and with which justifications? Should—or in some systems must—the court follow the legal analysis in other cases? They are part of a judicial structure based on the allocation of authority among institutions, and judges are often evaluated by how they use authority. This requires that they carefully compare new fact situations with prior decisions. In some systems (primarily common law jurisdictions) a court's decision may be legally "binding" on subsequent courts, so the authority is formal. In others, authority is less formal— that is, earlier decisions of a relevant court serve merely to guide later decisions.

Courts also use cases for the pragmatic purpose of increasing the consistency of decisions. They typically want to be seen as fair, and one element in the perception of fairness is whether an institution is consistent in the way it treats similar fact patterns. Here the legal reasoning of prior cases tends to be less important than aligning the facts of new cases with those in existing cases. CAs are often legally required to follow statutory language as interpreted in prior litigation, but they also have incentives to pay careful attention to comparing facts in order to be consistent in their decisions. All CAs can be expected to follow their own recent prior decisions, so these are particularly useful guides to predicting its decisions (except perhaps where a major political change occurs).

Particularly in newer systems, decision-makers may seek authority or guidance by referring to decisions from other jurisdictions that are considered to have high status, primarily those from the US and Europe.

3. USING ECONOMICS

Economic science is used in several ways. One is to identify the likely economic consequences of the conduct at issue. A second is to guide the application of legal principles by identifying whether and to what extent they are consistent with economic reasoning. In some competition law regimes, this guidance is highly influential, while in others its role is marginal. A third use goes further. It allows economics to provide the competition law norms themselves—that is, it allows economics to determine whether conduct violates the law. In US antitrust, for example, if conduct is "anti-competitive" according to economic analysis, it is generally considered a violation. If not, it is unlikely to be considered a violation.

Much depends on the degree of economic sophistication of the decision-maker. In a few regimes (e.g., US and EU) CAs rely on PhD-level economists who often use highly technical tools to analyze factual claims. Economists are expensive, however, and most regimes use less highly trained officials and engage in more basic forms of economic analysis. One clue for assessing the role accorded to economics in CAs is to review the educational background of the leading figures in the CA. A larger number of PhD economists suggests, for example, that economics will play a key role in decision-making.

Judges generally rely on their legal skills and experience in deciding cases, but in competition law they may take economic reasoning and conclusions into account. How a particular court will do this may be difficult to predict. Judges rarely have extensive knowledge of economics, so they must rely on simplified presentations of the results of economic analysis presented by "economic experts." These presentations become evidence, and they are evaluated according to standard judicial practices. Lawyers play a key role in making the results of economic analysis under-standable and convincing for judges and other legal professionals.

E. COERCION AND PRESSURE

Foreign governments and international institutions sometimes exert pressure on a government to enact competition law with particular characteristics or on a CA to implement the law in par-ticular ways. The greater these influences are, the less influence stated goals and identifiable methods have on decisions.

Sometimes these influences are direct and obvious. For ex-ample, during the 1990s the World Bank required many devel-oping countries to enact competition laws in order to receive much-needed loans. Pressure can also be less direct. A foreign government may, for example, provide financial support, exper-tise, enforcement assistance, and educational opportunities to a CA (or its leaders) in order to induce it to follow specific policies or practices. The US, the EU, Japan, and others have all used these strategies.

In some competition law regimes, these inducements invite corruption, so there it is often valuable to be aware of this possi-bility. The potential for corruption is particularly high in compe-tition law, because its targets are often large firms with extensive resources. The risk tends to be most acute where CAs are poorly funded, the rules and principles are unclear, or the CA has lim-ited independence. Even in stable, highly developed competition law regimes, however, the desire for personal gain can influence decision makers and subvert the stated goals of competition law.

In this chapter we have seen how institutions and methods shape the path from goals to decisions. We next turn to competi-tion law's targets.

PART II

COMPETITION LAW'S TARGETS

Part I examined the basic elements of competition law. This part puts them "in action." It identifies the conduct that competition laws seek to deter and the ways they pursue their targets. All regimes pursue the same basic types of conduct, but each identifies harmful conduct for itself and pursues targets in its own ways. We ask the same basic questions for each type of conduct. Why is it targeted? What tools (e.g., penalties and procedures) are used to deter it? And what factors influence how the tools are used?

Identifying harm: Why is it considered harmful? Basic answer: Because it interferes with competition law's goals. Chapter 3 reviewed these goals. Here we see how they are used to identify specific targets.

Specifying the target: Typically, a statute provides a general description of the targeted conduct, and the courts and/or the Competition Authority (CA) further specify the targets in regulations, guidelines, and court opinions. The more general the legislation, the greater the amount of discretion they have to do this.

Specific industries and groups are often exempted from the application of competition law, usually because they are subject to separate laws regulating their conduct. Banking, insurance, telecommunications, and sports are among the most common industry exemptions. Other exemptions are based on unique features of a country's circumstances or history. For example, South Africa's competition law provides certain exemptions for firms owned by "historically disadvantaged" social groups—that is, victims of the country's apartheid policies.

Pursuing the targets: How and to what extent a target is pursued depends primarily on the procedures, rules, resources, and incentives of the institution. In deciding whether to pursue conduct a CA will typically weigh its perceived benefits to society against its costs of pursuit, considering also the likelihood that the pursuit will deter the target conduct. The benefit to society can be measured by the harm the conduct causes. A CA will generally avoid using its resources to pursue conduct that causes limited or uncertain harm or the cost of pursuit would be high in relation to the harm.

It will consider both direct and indirect costs. Direct costs are the resources used to pursue the target—for example, employee salaries. It will also consider whether pursuing the target may bring its own harms to competition—for example, by deterring potentially beneficial conduct such as innovation. These are more difficult to assess, but they are often significant. Other factors such as general economic policy priorities (or even personal objectives) may also influence pursuit decisions.

Global patterns: Each target has a global profile—that is, patterns that help us know what to expect and how to evaluate what we find. For example, competition laws in emerging market countries tend to face at least some similar concerns, so they often have identifiable patterns in their choice of targets and in their decisions about pursuing them. Recognizing these patterns can greatly increase our understanding of the shared problems and responses, making information about one regime useful for understanding and predicting others that share the same pattern.

5

ANTICOMPETITIVE AGREEMENTS

Business firms make agreements for a variety of purposes. Most contribute to the effectiveness and value of markets, but some have the opposite effect. They reduce or distort competition rather than facilitate and support it. When they do, they can become targets of competition law.

Competition law focuses on two types of anticompetitive agreement. One includes agreements between competitors—referred to as "horizontal," because the parties operate in the same market and thus on the same level. Virtually all competition laws target and pursue them, and there is widespread agreement that they typically harm competition. The other type includes "vertical" agreements—those between firms that do not compete with each other, but perform different functions in bringing a particular product or service to market. They can also harm competition, but their effects are far more difficult to assess, and competition laws differ greatly in evaluating them. We will see why. These categories are becoming somewhat blurred by the Big Data issues we look at in Chapter 12, but they are still routinely used for most purposes.

The term "agreement" can be misleading, so we need to clarify two points. First, the form of agreement is usually irrelevant. An informal oral agreement can have the same legal consequences as a written one. In some competition laws, especially in the past and in emerging market regimes, competition laws have been applied only to agreements that have a particular form, but form requirements are often easily circumvented, and they have been eliminated from most systems. Second, the concept of "agreement" is far broader than many assume it to be. If firms intentionally act together (concerted action) to achieve a market outcome, that is usually enough to be considered an agreement for competition law purposes, although some competition laws require more tangible evidence of agreement. Competition laws are concerned

Competition Law and Antitrust. David J. Gerber, Oxford University Press (2020). © David J. Gerber.
DOI: 10.1093/oso/9780198727477.001.0001

with the intentional coordination of market conduct, regardless of how it is achieved. As we shall see, this can be a tricky issue. We look first at the treatment of horizontal agreements.

A. AGREEMENTS AMONG COMPETITORS (HORIZONTAL AGREEMENTS—CARTELS)

In March, 2019, the Chilean Competition Tribunal (TDLC) determined that three supermarket chains, Cencosud, SMU, and Wal-Mart, violated Article 3 of Decree Law No. 211 when they entered into an anticompetitive agreement covering the sale of fresh chicken meat. Specifically, these three chains were found to have colluded to maintain a minimum sales price for chicken meat that was equal to or higher than its wholesale price plus the value added tax. The tribunal found that the three chains together had significant market power to achieve this price increase. It also found that the objective of the collusion was to regulate the market and prevent a price war. Evidence was presented that the chains had a reporting mechanism in place which allowed members of the group to check on sales by other members of the group and punish suppliers who violated the agreement. On the basis of these findings, the TDLC imposed significant fines on each of the three companies involved.[1]

What's wrong with a simple agreement among competitors that is intended to avoid a price war that could harm the producers, their employees, and perhaps the economy of a town, city, or region? The question has often been asked in the past in relation to competition law, but it is seldom asked today. We will see why. Agreements among competitors are extremely common, because they can increase the prices on the market and thereby increase the profits of the participants. Why does the tribunal look closely at the combined market power of the participants? Do the parties have to agree in writing to such an agreement? Do they have to agree with each other in any formal sense at all? What if they just send some messages to each other about their production plans, perhaps indicating a willingness to cooperate in some way? Does that constitute an agreement for purposes of competition law and thus subject the companies to large fines and the parties responsible to possible terms in prison? The parties to such an "agreement" will try to keep it a secret, so how does a Competition Authority (CA) find out about it? Is evidence that the parties monitored each other's sales and the prices they charged sufficient to prove an "agreement"? Can governments entice participants to report such an agreement? If so, how?

Agreements among competitors (sometimes called "cartel agreements") are typically a central target of competition law. Where firms on the same market coordinate their market activities rather than compete, they reduce or eliminate the competition between them. If their combined share of the market is large enough, they can also reduce or even eliminate competition throughout the market. Competition laws differ, however, in the ways they identify the harm, in the importance they attach to it, and in the tools they use to combat it.

1. USES OF HORIZONTAL AGREEMENTS

Competitors agree to eliminate elements of competition between them for one basic reason: to achieve higher profits. For example, if all or most of the firms on a market agree not to compete with each other regarding the price of a product—let's say a television, each reduces or eliminates the risk that others will lower their prices in order to sell more televisions. Each is then in a position to sell its televisions at a higher price than otherwise would be possible. Some agreements among competitors may eventually benefit competition as well as benefitting the parties themselves—for example, where the agreement helps to foster innovation, but the ultimate goal of the parties is higher profits.

The effect of the strategy depends, however, on *how much of the market* is covered by the agreement! If the parties' combined market share is only 1 percent, the agreement will not achieve its objective of raising price, because firms that are not parties to the agreement will continue to compete on price, and purchasers will tend to buy from firms that offer lower prices. In this scenario, the participating firms do not have sufficient "market power" to influence the price on the market.

Where the agreement covers a large enough share of the market to influence price, the parties can raise their prices above a competitive price, reduce their output in support of the higher price, and thereby increase their profits. They sell less and make more; consumers buy less and pay more. Cartel members incur costs in organizing and policing such an agreement, but the potential gains often outweigh such costs, making such agreements very common.

Competitors can also achieve this objective by eliminating other forms of competition. They may, for example, divide territories among themselves (territorial market division) so that each participant supplies its own territory and need not be concerned with competition from the others. They may also agree on who will sell to particular types of customers or for particular uses of the product (customer market division). In another strategy, they agree to use their combined influence to reduce supplies or sales opportunities to firms that are not party to the agreement (group boycott). These agreements can have the same effect as a price agreement—namely, to allow firms to raise prices or reduce costs.

2. IDENTIFYING HARM

Each of the perspectives used to identify harm (see Ch. 3) recognizes the potential harm in such agreements:

Economic effects: They increase prices above a competitive level and thus undermine the efficiency of a market and reduce consumer welfare.

Political and social effects: They transfer wealth from consumers to producers, making them unfair to consumers and potentially contributing to income inequality and social disruptions.

Economic freedom: They limit the freedom of their members to compete.

Development impacts: They can also inhibit economic development by, for example, reducing incentives for domestic firms to develop new products.

3. TARGETING
CARTELS: SUBSTANTIVE LAW

Competition statutes typically contain general language that prohibits or otherwise penalizes agreements that "restrain trade" or "reduce competition." These broad provisions must be given more specific content, however, because all contracts can "restrain trade" in some sense, so laws often contain some procedure for targeting only those agreements that cause sufficient harm to warrant prohibition. This involves "balancing"—comparing the amount of harm caused by the agreement with any potential benefits it may have for competition or for the society more generally. US antitrust has long used the concept of "rule of reason" to perform this balancing function. In general, it requires that harm to competition be weighed against the agreement's procompetitive effects. The term (often untranslated) is frequently used in other systems to refer to balancing issues (although it is often used in ways that only vaguely resemble its US use). EU competition law balances these factors by providing exemptions for agreements that meet certain conditions. This significantly narrows the reach of the general prohibition of such agreements.

Where a cartel agreement's sole objective is to benefit its participants, there is seldom need for balancing. This is a "naked" or "hard core" cartel. A prime example is "price-fixing"—that is, agreements among competitors to charge essentially the same price for a specific product or service. Firms sometimes argue that these agreements stabilize prices and are therefore justified by the economic and political stability that is thought to result. This argument has occasionally been successful, especially in periods of economic stress and in countries facing significant instability, but this is uncommon. The "naked agreement" label often also includes the division of markets and group boycotts in which competitors agree to take concerted action to eliminate or discipline competitors who are not party to the agreement.

Balancing becomes more important where an agreement may also provide public benefits. For example, an agreement among competitors to engage in a joint research and development project to create a new cancer drug limits competition among the participants, but it is also intended to produce a new item of competition and thus provide benefits that outweigh its harms. Such projects are often very expensive and difficult to organize, and collaboration among competitors may therefore be necessary in order to obtain these public benefits.

Exemptions: Most competition statutes exempt certain types of cartels. It is common, for example, to exempt so-called "de minimis" agreements in which the market shares of the participants and/or the value of the agreement is so small that it is highly unlikely to harm competition. Some systems also use cartel exemptions to promote the competitive opportunities of small and medium-sized businesses on the grounds that allowing the firms to cooperate may enable them to prosper and perhaps compete with larger firms, especially foreign ones, and on world markets.

4. DETECTING CARTEL AGREEMENTS

A CA can only combat horizontal agreements if it learns about them, but they are often difficult to detect. First, they are often based on informal and indirect communications. Managers may merely exchange information about their intended output during informal discussions. This may not look like an agreement, but, as noted above, the issue in competition law is whether the parties have intentionally coordinated their market conduct, and an exchange of information may constitute such coordination. Second, the parties are likely to conceal such an agreement as much as possible, knowing that it may be illegal in one or more relevant jurisdiction. Third, those who compete with cartel members are unlikely to reveal the cartel. If the agreement succeeds in raising the price of a good on the market, non-members benefit from the price increase at least as much as the members themselves. Finally, consumers harmed by a cartel may notice price increases and suspect a cartel, but they are unlikely to have both sufficient information to identify it and sufficient incentives and resources to take action against it.

Two main tools are used to detect cartels. One is to trawl for them. The CA can review market statistics such as price behavior or it may ask market participants or foreign CAs for information. This may reveal patterns that indicate cartel activity—such as parallel price changes, but cartel arrangements are very common, and trawling can only reveal a small percentage of them. Moreover, the process is costly and often an inefficient use of a CA's resources.

A more productive and efficient strategy is a leniency program. Such programs create incentives for cartel participants to reveal the cartel in which they are participating. The government basically says, "If you tell us about your cartel, we will exempt you from most or all potential penalties for participating in it." This allows a cartel member to avoid or limit the sanctions that the other cartel members face. These programs emerged in US anti-trust law in the 1990s and have since become a key feature of cartel enforcement in all major competition law regimes. For many CAs they represent the only effective means of detecting cartels and acquiring the evidence necessary to pursue them.

Leniency programs are widespread, and their details vary significantly. (1) *Eligibility*: some offer leniency only to the first party to report a cartel, while others provide partial leniency for others who provide information. (2) *Information required* from leniency applicants differs in amount and type. (3) *Enforcement value of information*: exemption is likely to be available only where the information has enough enforcement value to warrant it. This may mean, for example, that the information must enable a CA to identify the cartel and its members or that it must lead to proof sufficient to support sanctions against cartel members. Given that most major competition law regimes have leniency programs, a cartel participant must often take a global view in deciding if, where, and how to apply for leniency. This can be a very complicated assessment. These programs can also interact with private enforcement in highly complex ways. Lawyers for firms with transnational connections or operations have to be aware of filings around the world that may affect their clients, because leniency filings can open opportunities to assert private claims or require defensive measures to protect against such claims.

5. PURSUING CARTEL AGREEMENTS: BENEFITS AND COSTS

When a CA identifies a cartel, it typically assesses the amount of harm the agreement has caused, the costs of proving the harm and of using specific tools to pursue it, and the likely deterrent effect of using the tools.

Measuring harm: Measuring harm is often an imprecise enterprise, particularly where the harm is assessed in relation to social or political goals. How can the agreement's impact on social equality or economic freedom be measured? The decision-maker must often make very rough estimates. Measuring *economic* harm can provide greater precision, but even here many factors may make assessment difficult. Much depends on the CA's resources and on the training of its officials. In general, the greater the care used and the precision sought, the higher the costs. A CA that has more extensive resources can gather more factual information and engage in more sophisticated economic analysis than a CA that is smaller or has fewer resources. As a result, it may be in a position to measure harm with greater precision. Resources are especially important where rigorous economic analysis is expected to play a key role in the assessment.

Proving agreement: Proving the existence of an agreement can be a challenge. Recall that the issue here is whether the parties intentionally coordinate their market conduct, not whether they reach a formal agreement. Sometimes a CA may have little doubt that the parties coordinated their activities, but little proof that they actually did. A leniency program may yield sufficient proof, but if it does not, the CA may have to rely on circumstantial evidence such as price movements to infer agreement. Often, however, courts find this type of evidence insufficient.

Obstacles increase further where potentially relevant materials are located outside the pursuing jurisdiction. This is one reason why parties often conclude cartel agreements in countries where there is little or no cartel enforcement. In particular, they often seek to avoid the reach of US antitrust law by meeting in other countries, because US law applies criminal penalties (including jail terms) to individuals considered responsible for the cartel. Relatively few others do.

Tools and costs: A CA usually has the same tools available for both horizontal and vertical agreements, but the benefits and costs of using them often differ significantly.

—**Prohibition and fines:** Statutes typically prohibit anticompetitive agreements and authorize penalties for violating the prohibition. In most regimes, fines are the most widely used tools. Cartel agreements typically incur the largest fines, because the harm is often apparent and cartel members can be expected to know that such agreements are illegal.

—**Contractual invalidity:** A finding that an agreement is anticompetitive typically makes that agreement invalid and unenforceable. This can itself be a major deterrent to cartel formation.

—**Criminal sanctions:** A few systems also provide criminal sanctions, including jail terms, against individuals responsible for such agreements, again on the grounds that they knowingly violated the law. They are considered an important deterrent under US antitrust law, but they are less often used elsewhere. In general, criminal penalties are only imposed on horizontal agreements that are considered "naked"—that is, with no function other than to enrich the participants.

Potential deterrent effects: Widespread awareness of the harm that cartel agreements can cause gives CAs incentives to use the full range of enforcement tools against them. Despite their efforts, however, the lure of potential gain for participants makes cartels common. The greater the enforcement efforts, the greater the incentive for participants to conceal them.

6. GLOBAL DIMENSIONS

The general perception that cartels are harmful aligns the interests of cartel enforcers around the globe, but the intensity of pursuit varies. In systems that focus primarily on economic harm, cartels tend to be the focus of enforcement, largely because the harm is obvious and because economics can assess it with a high degree of confidence. Where the focus is on other types of harm, cartel enforcement may be less central. In emerging market jurisdictions, for example, enforcers must consider the interests of domestic producers and may accordingly pay less attention to cartels and greater attention to unilateral conduct and mergers. This concern also leads to official and unofficial exemptions for many types of horizontal agreements, especially among small and medium-sized domestic firms.

B. AGREEMENTS AMONG NON-COMPETITORS (VERTICAL AGREEMENTS)

In August, 2013, the Shanghai High People's Court found that an agreement implemented by Johnson & Johnson Medical Equipment Company (Shanghai) and Johnson & Johnson Medical Equipment Company

*(China), collectively "Johnson & Johnson," eliminated and restricted compe-
tition, rendering the agreement a monopoly agreement in violation of Article
14 of the Chinese Antimonopoly Law (AML). Specifically, the agreement prevented one of Johnson & Johnson's medical equipment distributors,
formally known as Beijing Ruibang Yonghe Equipment Technology and
Trading Company and informally known as "Rainbow," from selling
products outside of a designated territory as well as selling products at a price
lower than the price set by Johnson & Johnson. This is "resale price maintenance" or "vertical price fixing." The language of the AML seemed to
state that such agreements were "per se" illegal, but the court claimed that
the agreement should not be considered illegal without analysis of its effects.
It proceeded to consider the agreement's effects on competition and concluded
that Johnson & Johnson had the market power to control prices and that the
agreement's anticompetitive effects outweighed its procompetitive effects.
The agreement was, therefore, illegal.[2]*

*A multinational manufacturing company based in the US wants to dis-
tribute its products in China and chooses to do so by establishing subsidiary companies there. It just wants to control where the distributors sell the
products and the prices at which they sell them. This is a very common arrangement both within individual countries and across the globe. What can
be harmful about that? As we shall see, some competition law regimes usually see harm in such arrangements while others seldom see such harm. Why
the difference? Does the court's analysis of market power have anything to
do with it? Does it depend on what the law is looking at? If the central legal
question is whether the agreement restricts the freedom of the distributor to
compete, the answer is clearly "yes." That is its stated objective. But if the
issue is whether the agreement increases the price of the product to the consumer, the answer isn't so simple. It becomes necessary to analyze the effects
of the agreement on consumers, and that analysis is likely to focus on the
controlling firm's market power. Do you think that the competition law of a
large, wealthy country whose firms often control companies in other countries
is likely to be more or less concerned about this type of arrangement than a
smaller country that depends on foreign investment? Why?*

Agreements between firms that are only related to each other
vertically—for example, through distribution or marketing

---

[2] Beijing Ruibang Yonghe Kemao Youian Gongsi Su Qiangsheng (Shanghai)
Yiliao Qicai Youxian Gongsi Deng Zongxiang Longduan Xieyi Jiufen An [Beijing
Ruibang Yonghe Equipment Technology & Trading Co. Ltd. ("Rainbow")
v. Johnson & Johnson (Shanghai) Medical Equipment Co. Ltd. et al.] (Shanghai
High People's Ct. August 1, 2013) CLI.C.6234448 (Lawinfochina).

obligations—can also harm competition, but laws diverge sharply in the ways they identify, evaluate, and treat such agreements. Some actively combat them, while others pay little attention to them. These differences are a major source of uncertainty and costs for firms operating across borders, and they often lead to misunderstandings, mistakes, and conflicts.

A vertical agreement limits the freedom to compete of one or more of the parties, but unlike horizontal agreements the parties here are not competitors. They perform different functions on the path of a specific product or service from producer to consumer. The agreement does limit the freedom of one or more of the parties to compete, so it may limit *intrabrand competition*—that is, competition between participants dealing with the *same brand*. It does not necessarily influence competition among brands—that is, *interbrand competition*, which is the competition that can increase or lower prices to consumers. As a result, if the competition law is concerned only with the effect of an agreement on consumers, the restraints imposed on the controlled party may be irrelevant. We will see what these terms mean and why the difference between interbrand and intrabrand competition is so important.

1. USES AND CONTEXTS OF VERTICAL AGREEMENTS

In a typical vertical agreement, a manufacturer agrees to sell its products to a distributor and specifies the distributor's obligations relating to resale of the product. For example, the agreement may obligate the distributor to sell the product only at a price designated by the producer ("resale price maintenance") or only in a specified geographical area or only to specific types of customers. This may restrict competition among distributors of the product. The distributor may also be required to provide specified services (e.g., repair services) to purchasers of the product.

The agreement gives the producer a degree of control over how its products will be distributed and sold without having to perform these functions itself. It can gain the cost-saving benefits of integrating economic functions without owning the units that distribute the product. This *integrates functions by contract rather than through ownership*. In exchange, the distributor acquires the right to sell the products and often to receive other forms of support from the manufacturer. The agreement provides value for both parties.

Vertical agreements are particularly common where there are obstacles to integration by ownership. For example, where there is limited access to capital, firms often do not have the resources to perform multiple functions, so firms may not be in a position to acquire financing to integrate through ownership. Integration by contract provides an alternative means of integrating these functions and improving profitability and perhaps promoting economic development.

Obstacles to integration by ownership were common almost everywhere until the rise of the modern mega-corporation, which began in Europe, the US, and Japan in the late nineteenth century. Increased access to capital, improved communication and transportation technology, and changed legal and political environments have, however, reduced these obstacles in some countries making vertical agreements seem relatively benign. This, in turn, has shifted competition law attention away from them in some regimes (e.g., the US.) In emerging markets and smaller economies, however, concerns about these harms often remain strong. Here restrictions on the competitive freedom of smaller firms are often seen as giving excessive influence to manufacturers and large distributors. The issue is often politically sensitive, particularly where it implicates foreign influence and/or class divisions.

Globalization adds complexity to the picture by making it more likely that the parties to a vertical agreement will be *located in different countries*. For example, a firm in country A may supply component parts, a firm in country B may manufacture the goods, a firm in country C may arrange for distribution, and firms in country D may sell the products to consumers. This is a global supply (or value) chain. They have become an important part of the global economic picture, but they pose new challenges for competition law. One example: if a manufacturer in country B uses a vertical agreement to control the conduct of a distributor in C, the agreement may violate C's competition law, but not the competition laws of countries B or D. This can create uncertainty, confusion, and wasted effort. Governments in emerging markets are sometimes highly sensitive to the problems such a scenario creates, but a transborder legal framework for dealing with them has yet to emerge.

This scenario highlights a central theme in the law relating to vertical agreements—the potential for conflict: between large and small firms—between manufacturers and distributors—and between competition laws of different countries. Producers typically want to control the distribution and sale of their products, while those they control typically wish to maintain maximum freedom from such controls. Competition law is often used to deal with these conflicts, but there is limited agreement about whether and how this can be done.

2. IDENTIFYING HARM

Identifying harm in vertical agreements is complicated, uncertain, and often controversial. Some see harm as highly unlikely, while others consider it a significant threat to markets and even to society. Recognizing the methods they use is the key to understanding these contrasting views.

Economic effects: Economic effects are often difficult to discern, because they depend on numerous factors such as the amount of competition covered by the agreement, the structure of the markets involved, and the relative economic position of the participants in those markets. For example, if a distribution agreement between a manufacturer that has a dominant position in its market and each of its distributors requires that products be sold at a specific price, the agreement may eliminate price competition on some markets. If, however, the manufacturer does not have a dominant position, the provision may have little or no effect. An economic analysis is necessary to determine its impact. This complexity and uncertainty leads regimes that rely on economic analysis to be cautious about identifying harm. Categorizing particular conduct as a violation often makes little sense, because the same conduct may cause harmful effects in one context, but no effects in another. The effects on innovation and economic development are equally or more uncertain.

Economic freedom: Where the goal is economic freedom, a vertical restraint may be harmful, because it necessarily limits the freedom to compete of one or more of the parties. Applying this analysis faces many hurdles: there is no clear way of deciding when a restriction "has gone too far" in reducing economic freedom and whether it can be justified.

Social-political harms: Vertical agreements involve control. Typically, a larger manufacturing firm controls smaller distributors and retailers. The smaller firms may agree to the arrangement, but the power disparities lead to concerns that it may be unfair to smaller and economically weaker distributors and retailers. Concerns about power increase where the controlling player is located in a high-income country, but the controlled firm is located in an emerging market. This often leads officials in emerging markets to pay close attention to such agreements. We will see this issue again in the following chapter which focuses on powerful firms acting alone.

3. SPECIFYING THE TARGET

Many statutes do not distinguish between horizontal and vertical agreements. They use the same general terms to refer to both. This can lead to confusion. Issues pertinent to horizontal agreements may, for example, be mistakenly or misleadingly applied to vertical agreements. It is often valuable to recognize when this mixing inhabits a discussion or judicial opinion.

There are, however, many other statutes that specify particular types of vertical restraints as violations. Prominent among these are resale price maintenance provisions, tying arrangements (tying the purchase of one product to the purchase of another), requirements that a distributor deal only in the goods of the manufacturer (exclusive dealing), and territorial and customer restrictions on distributors and retailers. This has the advantage of providing clearer guidance to firms, and it allows courts and CAs to use standard legal methods to apply the law. Statutes of this type are particularly common in emerging markets, where CAs typically cannot accommodate the cost of applying extensive analysis and where many see advantages in making clear to foreign firms what they should avoid. Yet, as we have just noted, it can also prohibit agreements that have no anticompetitive effect. As a result, CAs and some courts look beyond the apparently clear prohibition in the statute and consider the effects of the agreement (see example above). A statutory prohibition may, therefore, not actually be treated as a prohibition, which makes it important to look beyond formal claims in this area.

4. DETECTION AND PROOF

Vertical agreements are extremely common, and many go undetected. Most are of minor importance and attract limited enforcement attention. Where an agreement violates a specific statutory provision, a CA may in some legal systems be obligated to pursue it, but otherwise it will assess its potential harm in relation to the cost of pursuit and the likelihood of deterrence.

5. THE DECISION TO PURSUE: TOOLS AND COSTS

Enforcement tools used to pursue vertical agreements are basically the same as those used for horizontal agreements. Fines are common, but criminal penalties are virtually never used in such cases, largely because the parties may be unaware that the agreement is unlawful. Where private enforcement is available, vertical restraints cases are often prominent. These agreements tend to create dependency relationships, so if a manufacturer terminates such an agreement, the result may be devastating for the distributor, who will often sue the manufacturer for the harm caused by the termination. Competition law issues are often at the center of these controversies.

Where rules regarding vertical restraints are clear and enforced, they can have a significant deterrent effect. Where an effects-based analysis is used, however, both public and private enforcement efforts can be impaired by the uncertainty and costs of enforcement.

6. GLOBAL PATTERNS AND DYNAMICS

A sharp conflict shapes the global landscape relating to vertical restraints. One group of jurisdictions relies at least to some extent on specific rules that designate particular restraints as illegal.

CAs and courts interpret and apply these laws using traditional forms of legal analysis. This form-based approach is relatively inexpensive and thus particularly appealing where a CA's resources are limited. Moreover, it appeals to those who value predictability and those who support extensive enforcement of competition law. A second group relies on economic analysis to determine whether the agreements harm competition. Regimes in this group emphasize the risks of over-enforcement posed by form-based analysis and accord less importance to the need for predictability. US antitrust law is based on this view, and its representatives often urge its acceptance by others. Each approach reflects a combination of historical factors, considerations of economic policy, and political pressures. Each also provides benefits and disadvantages for particular groups as well as for particular countries. The differences play out against a background of disparities in power and wealth between "high income" countries that tend to favor more economics-based analysis and those with fewer resources, which rely more heavily on specific statutory language. Recognizing this play of forces is highly valuable for negotiating the global landscape.

6

DOMINANT FIRM UNILATERAL CONDUCT: MONOPOLIZATION AND ABUSE OF DOMINANCE

The European Commission concluded in 2017 that Google had infringed Article 102 of the relevant EU treaty (TFEU) and Article 54 of the Agreement on the European Economic Area ("EEA Agreement") when it displayed its own comparison-shopping service more favorably than competing comparison-shopping services on its general search results pages. It found that Google held a dominant position under Article 102, which prohibits a firm from abusing its dominant position, and that it abused its dominant position in thirteen separate national markets by directing online traffic toward its own comparison-shopping service and diverting it from competing comparison-shopping services.[1] It did not engage in extensive economic analysis of the effects of the conduct on consumers.

In contrast, the United States Court of Appeals for the Tenth Circuit did engage in economic analysis when it concluded that Microsoft, the leading provider of intel-compatible personal computer operating systems, did not engage in anti-competitive conduct under section 2 of the Sherman Antitrust Act when it withdrew access to its namespace extensions from independent software vendors after first offering to share access.[2] The court based its conclusion in large part on a finding that no evidence had been presented to prove that Microsoft was willing to sacrifice short-term profits or to irrationally harm competition.

In both cases the issue is whether a single firm acting unilaterally violated the relevant competition law provision. The EU decision rested on the concept of abuse of power. The EU Commission said that Google used its power to distort and interfere with competition to its own benefit. In the US case, the court focused on the economic rationality of Microsoft's conduct and concluded that the conduct was not irrational and therefore not a violation of the US law condemning "monopolization." The differing perspectives play important roles in the global competition law arena. Why are there such

---

[1] European Commission Decision (June 27, 2017) *CASE AT.39740 Google Search (Shopping)* ANTITRUST PROCEDURE.

[2] Novell, Inc. v. Microsoft Corp., 731 F.3d 1064 (10th Cir. 2013).

Competition Law and Antitrust. David J. Gerber, Oxford University Press (2020). © David J. Gerber.
DOI: 10.1093/oso/9780198727477.001.0001

major differences between competition laws? History? Politics? Ideology? Characteristics of the national economy, particularly in relation to global markets? All of the above? Single-firm conduct is generally considered to be especially difficult to analyze in competition law. We will see why.

The above examples feature the conduct of a single firm acting unilaterally—that is, by itself. If a firm has sufficient influence or "power" on a market, it can exclude rivals or limit their capacity to compete and thereby significantly harm competition. Here the harm does not result from a specific agreement (as in Ch. 5) but from the conduct of a single firm. Most competition law statutes target this type of conduct, but there are important variations in actual treatment, and virtually all systems struggle to respond to it effectively.

This component of competition law is often controversial and politically sensitive. It typically involves large firms, many of which are also politically influential. Their power—whether imagined or not—often elicits fear, resentment, and envy, and this fuels efforts to use competition law to combat their threats. The area symbolizes and crystalizes the conflict between the public interest and private economic power, and it touches on major social and political issues such as inequality, political freedom, and democracy.

Globalization adds a further dimension to the tension. Dominant firms are typically based in high income countries (often the US or Europe) but the harm is often related to firms and consumers in poorer and weaker countries. As financial resources have become increasingly concentrated and large firms have expanded their influence on geographical and digital markets, the governments in poorer countries have sought ways to limit the potential harms.

A. POWER AS THE STARTING POINT

Analysis of unilateral conduct starts from the premise that a dominant firm's influence on a market makes certain kinds of conduct harmful even though the same conduct by a firm without such power may be harmless. For example, if a firm with a 1 percent market share sells below its cost of production, the price reduction is probably not a competition law issue, because it cannot influence the rest of the market. If, on the other hand, a firm with an 85 percent market share engages in the same conduct, the conduct may drive competitors from the market or dissuade other firms from entering it.

Where a firm has a large enough share of the market to influence by itself how the market functions, it is considered "dominant" and/or said to have "monopoly power." It is this power that allows it to act in ways that a firm that is subject to competition could not act (at least not without losing money). Crucially, this power *relates to a specific market*, so competition laws must identify or "define" the relevant market in order to assess power.

B. DEFINING THE MARKET

Market definition is the basis for assessing a firm's power. It is central to the analysis of unilateral conduct, so it is often a battle-ground in which plaintiffs seek narrow definitions and defendants seek the opposite. The broader the market, the smaller the influence of any firm's individual market share. For example, a producer of men's dress shoes may have a large enough market share to create dominance in the market for men's dress shoes, but if the market is defined to include all shoes, its share of the market may be too small for it to have influence.

The goal of market definition is to identify the firms that are competing with each other. A market may be defined by geography—for example, are two stores ten miles apart competing for the same customers? If yes, they are considered part of the same geographical market. It may also be defined in relation to a product or service—is product A competing with product B for the same customers? If so, they are part of the same product market. In some cases, the competitive relationship may be based on a product's use—are firms competing to be used for a particular purpose?

There is no fixed formula for defining a market, but the basic idea is that firms are competing where the market conduct of one influences what its competitors can do. Competition laws use various indicators to assess the scope of the relevant market. One asks what happens to the demand for product A if product B's price changes. If B's price changes and there is no change in demand for product A, the two firms are probably not competing, because potential buyers of product B are not switching to product A. If, on the other hand, demand for product A increases when B's price increases, this is evidence that consumers are responding to B's price increase by switching to product A, so they are in the same market. It is not quite so simple, but for our purposes this suffices.

Three basic methods are used to measure this sensitivity. One is to conduct market surveys which ask consumers, for example, "Would you switch from product A to product B if A were to increase in price by a given percentage." A second is to analyze past patterns in similar situations to predict what is likely to happen in the future. The third is to use economic modeling to identify the probable incentives of consumers. Each method involves a different set of costs, and this can influence the choices institutions make in using them. Each method is imperfect, so two or more may be used together in defining the market. Where the conduct has already occurred, this data is usually seen as reasonably dependable. Where the issue is the future effect of the conduct, as in merger analysis (Ch. 7) the data is considered less reliable, because markets evolve, often rapidly, and past responses become less useful in predicting future ones.

Market definition is notoriously frustrating. Many lawyers, administrators, and judges complain that it is uncertain and often seems arbitrary. The methods used are necessarily imprecise, because many factors can influence consumer behavior and because it is difficult to predict how a particular decision-maker will define a market. Experienced practitioners often study the factors that a particular Competition Authority (CA) or court has considered important in the very recent past as a basis for predicting what it will do in the future.

C. DOMINANCE AND
MONOPOLY POWER

Market share is generally used as the primary indicator of power. This generally refers to the percentage that a supplier's sales have of the total sales on the market. Laws vary as to how much market share constitutes dominance in various contexts. Some regimes (e.g., South Africa) specify the market share percentage that is deemed to constitute dominance. Others assess the necessary market share more flexibly. Some may require 60 percent; others may find it at much lower levels. Much depends on the market's structure—that is, how the market shares of other participants are arrayed. For example, in a highly concentrated market in which each of three firms has a 30 percent market share, competition between the three may be intense—no firm has power over price. In contrast, a 30 percent market share may be enough to control a market in which no other firm has more than a 2 percent share. Some CAs provide guidelines that explain how they assess dominance. Some (e.g., India) require that the social obligations and costs of the firm be taken into account in assessing dominance.

D. THE MOST
COMMON CONDUCT
STANDARD: EXCLUSION

Possessing power is rarely seen as a competition law violation; some form of conduct is also required. As we know, a regime's goals shape its conduct standards. Where economic goals are central, the focus is usually on whether the conduct is "exclusionary." Where political and social goals are considered, issues such as economic freedom and effects on income equality are often considered.

Exclusionary conduct exists where a dominant firm excludes a competitor from a market or impedes its capacity to compete effectively—for example, by using its power to interfere with a rival's supply arrangements and thereby increasing its costs and reducing its capacity to compete. Economic analysis is used to assess whether the conduct has led to an increase in price over a competitive price or had another similar impact on market competition. Types of exclusionary conduct include: predatory pricing, unilateral boycotts, refusal to deal, bundling or tying of products, and others.

The example of predatory pricing illustrates some of the issues involved. If a dominant firm reduces its prices below its cost of production in order to drive competitors out of the market, reduce their incentive or capacity to compete, or deter potential new entrants from entering the market, it may reduce competition. This is predatory pricing and violates most competition laws. The underlying assumption is that a dominant firm has a strong enough market position to take short-term losses in order to achieve long-term anticompetitive gains, so this conduct may be rational from the firm's standpoint and effective as a competitive strategy. A weaker firm cannot effectively use the strategy, because if it reduces prices below cost, it will merely lose money! Systems differ in the measure of cost that is used to assess predation (some use average variable cost, e.g., while others use average total cost). In some systems additional concepts are used in the analysis. For example, in the US, the courts have generally accepted the idea that there must also be a rational expectation that the dominant firm can recoup its losses.

A central issue in the treatment of unilateral conduct from any perspective is that potentially anticompetitive conduct is embedded in and interwoven with other elements of a firm's overall business plan. This makes it difficult to isolate the harmful conduct with confidence and, especially, to assess damage resulting from it. Moreover, conduct that is permitted under competition law when a firm does not have monopoly power can become a violation as the firm acquires a dominant position, so there may be no clear beginning or ending of the harmful conduct. Microsoft, for example, started by giving away its software. As long as they did not have monopoly power, this was not an antitrust problem, but it became a potential violation when the firm did acquire monopoly power.

E. SAME CONDUCT
DIFFERENT NAMES

In the US and a few other countries, the term "monopoliza-tion" is used to describe harmful dominant firm conduct, while in Europe and elsewhere it is usually referred to as "abuse of a dominant position." This sometimes leads to confusion and un-certainty, but just be aware that the two labels refer to the same category of conduct—anticompetitive conduct by a single firm.

Monopolization: Section 2 of the US Sherman Act prohibits "monopolization" (see Ch. 8). The basic idea is that a single firm with monopoly power "monopolizes" when it excludes or hinders competitors or potential competitors in order to acquire control of a market or increase its control of a market, but a cen-tury or so of judicial opinions interpreting the term has produced little clarity beyond that. This may be one reason why few other systems have chosen to use the concept.

Abuse of a dominant position: Most jurisdictions use this standard to assess unilateral conduct. It is clearer than "monopoli-zation" in that it specifies (1) that it applies only to dominant firms and (2) only to conduct that constitutes "abuse of dominance." Where it is used, courts and CAs have often been able to achieve at least a degree of clarity about how to use it.

F. A LESS COMMON CONDUCT
STANDARD: EXPLOITING
CONSUMERS

A second type of abuse involves "exploiting" consumers. Although many jurisdictions include it, some, including the US, do not. This refers to conduct in which a firm's dominance allows it to extract more from consumers than competition would allow, typically by raising its price above a competitive price. Its dominance is here used to "exploit" consumers. The concept was first used in German competition law during the early twentieth century, but it is now widespread in Europe, Latin America, and elsewhere.

The concept of exploitation abuse is often seen as politically attractive. The prospect of using competition law to reduce prices is often a source of political support, particularly where inflation is a major concern. It also directly addresses the threat of dominant firm power and sharply symbolizes the conflict between powerful firms and those subject to that power.

Yet many competition officials encounter two main obstacles that make it less attractive to apply. First, it calls for proof that the price exceeds a competitive price, but determining what the competitive price is or would be is necessarily speculative and therefore difficult to defend. Second, there is no clear and consistent way of deciding how much higher a firm's price must be in order to constitute abuse—2 percent? 5 percent? There have been many efforts to identify such principles, but few, if any, have been found widely convincing. As a result, this form of abuse is often criticized, especially in the US, as inherently discretionary and another name for price regulation. Where CAs or courts apply rigorous legal standards, this form of abuse is seldom enforced, because it is so hard to prove, although CAs sometimes use it as a threat to induce large firms (e.g., service station owners in Europe) to reduce their prices. This has become a big issue in the debates about competition law and Big Data (see Ch. 12).

G. PURSUING
UNILATERAL CONDUCT

The uncertainties in this area make decisions to pursue unilateral conduct risky and sometimes very expensive. As a result, public enforcement is typically limited, and private enforcement rare. Fines are usually the only tools available, but, assessing the amount of such fines tends to be highly uncertain. Criminal penalties are not used because holding a firm to an uncertain standard would be unfair (and in some systems unconstitutional). Where a reviewing court requires adequate proof of harm before approving a CA's decision, the CA's efforts are particularly vulnerable to reversal. This risk is lower where review is less strict. Political issues must also be considered. The lack of a clear basis for a decision opens a CA to the criticism that it based its decision on factors such as corruption or political influence. The fact that such cases often involve large, well-known firms with political leverage increases this concern and invites interference from the executive branch.

Deterrence potential is also difficult to estimate. Firms that dominate a market are typically large, and many are also well known—for example, Google. A CA that takes action against such a firm can be assured of publicity. This may deter other firms from considering similar conduct, but it may also draw unwanted attention to the CA and subject it to attacks. The CA's calculation is a difficult one.

H. ECONOMIC DEPENDENCE AND RELATIVE MARKET POWER

Firms that do not dominate a market may nevertheless have power over their suppliers or distributors. This has led some legislatures to create a distinct set of principles to deal with harm from the abuse of *relative* market power. Here harm results not from the effects of conduct on a market, but from its effects on one or more firms that are economically dependent on a powerful firm. The basic idea is that a firm may be able to impose conditions on dependent firms that impede their capacity to compete and thereby reduce competition. It is often also seen as simply unfair. Such legislation often gives dependent firms (usually suppliers of the dominant firm) a legal basis for claiming compensation for such harms from the firm that causes the harm. The idea was first discussed in the context of German competition law development, and it has spread to some other countries, mainly in Latin America and East Asia (e.g., Japan).[3] It is not part of US antitrust law.

---

[3] It was included Germany's Act Against Restraints of Competition ch. 2 § 20, Law of July 27, 1957, as amended 1965, 1973, 1976, 1980, 1989, 1998, 2005, 2013, and 2017; Japan's Act on Prohibition of Private Monopolization and Maintenance of Fair Trade (originally enacted as Act No. 54 of April 14, 1947).

I. GLOBAL PATTERNS
AND DYNAMICS

From a global perspective, the treatment of dominant firm conduct divides along several lines. One is more formal than actual—the line between states that use the concept of monopolization and those that use the abuse of dominance concepts. As noted above, this may make little difference in outcomes, but it is important to recognize that the two concepts relate to the same type of conduct and that the languages and logics used often differ significantly.

A second divide is far more significant. In systems that rely primarily or exclusively on economic analysis of effects, enforcement tends to be limited by the difficulty of proving the effects and by the uncertainty and cost of trying. Where political and social goals are also considered, however, enforcement sometimes proceeds without a firm or predictable legal base.

Finally, the interests of states in this area of competition law diverge significantly. Capital-exporting countries that are home to powerful companies often pay limited attention to unilateral conduct. Capital-importing countries (many of which are less economically robust) may have stronger incentives to pursue such conduct. In many countries, political support for competition law focuses on the conduct of powerful firms, and often the dominant firms are not domestic, but foreign.

7

MERGERS AND ACQUISITIONS

*In General Electric/Honeywell v. European Commission (2001), the
Commission blocked a proposed merger between two very large US
corporations – General Electric 2000 Merger Sub, Inc., a wholly owned
subsidiary of General Electric (GE), and Honeywell, Inc., which would
have resulted in Honeywell becoming a wholly owned subsidiary of GE. It
was probably the largest merger in history. The US competition authorities
approved the merger. The European Commission blocked it. After extensive
investigation of the local, regional, and global markets in which the parties
operated, the Commission concluded that GE had a dominant position in
several markets for various aircraft engines as well as having significant financial influence in these and other markets. Honeywell, it found, had significant advantages in several product markets because it could provide a range
of products that could not be matched by any other competitors. According to
the Commission, the merger would "bring about anti-competitive effects as
a result of horizontal overlaps and the vertical and conglomerate integration
of the merging parties activities." Specifically, the horizontal overlap would
amount to a 100 percent market share for the merged entity in some markets,
and it would enjoy "a significant financial and commercial advantage"
over its competitors, because it could then provide bundled and packaged
products that no other entity anywhere else in the world could provide. The
Commission specifically noted how certain customers, that is, airlines, would
have no choice but to buy certain products from the merged entity. As a result,
they could expect lower profits, which in turn would result in less investment
in research and development. Ultimately, these competitors would experience
market foreclosure and market exit, as they would be unable to compete with
the resulting merged entity. The focus was on harm to European markets and
their consumers.*[1]

*In May 2019, the Australian competition authority (Australian
Competition and Consumer Commission—ACCC) found that Pacific
National, an Australian firm active in transporting goods in a specific re-
gion of Australia, had violated Australia's competition statute by acquiring a*

---

[1] General Electric/Honeywell v. Commission (Case COMP/M.2220)
Commission Decision [2001] OJ (C331) 24.

Competition Law and Antitrust. David J. Gerber, Oxford University Press (2020). © David J. Gerber.
DOI: 10.1093/oso/9780198727477.001.0001

railroad terminal owned by a firm (Aurizon) that handled much of the trans-portation moving in and out of that region. The case involved arrangments between and in relation to "the supply of intermodal freight and bulk steel rail linehaul services to various end-users for whom transportation by road or sea was not an economically effective substitute." Specifically, the ACCC alleged that Pacific National's acquisition of the Acacia Ridge Terminal from Aurizon would have the effect of substantially lessening competition in breach of section 50 of the Competition and Consumer Act of 2010 (CCA). Also, the ACCC alleged that a "terminal services subcontract" between Pacific National and Aurizon that provided for Pacific National to conduct the day-to-day operations at the interstate side of the Acacia Ridge Terminal would essentially give Pacific National a monopoly over rail freight into north Queensland, in violation of section 45 of the CCA. Pacific National agreed, however, to provide undertakings that it would not discriminate against other rail operators who wanted to use the terminal, and, on that basis, the court ruled that the merger could take place.[2]

Acquisitions by large, well-known firms such as Google, Microsoft, and GE often receive extensive media coverage. That was certainly true of the GE/Honeywell example, but there are many other smaller mergers that gain few, if any, headlines. The Australian case is an example of such a smaller acquisition—a kind of "every day" arrangement. The firms were not global in size and scale of operations. It was in some ways typical of the kinds of arrangements made by firms everywhere to improve their ef-ficiency. The acquiring firm was seeking to integrate the terminal function into its distribution arrangements. It expected thereby to achieve savings in its operations and perhaps also improve its competitive position. Yet the re-sult would be a "near monopoly" of the "intermodal traffic" in the area, so the ACCC found a violation of the statute. The reviewing court accepted, however, an undertaking from the acquiring firm in which it promised to allow competing firms to use the terminal and approved the merger on that basis. Competition Authorities (CAs) and courts often recognize the po-tential economic value of a merger and seek to allow it subject to conditions. Here the approval was based on a "behavioral" remedy—one that would inevitably call for some degree of monitoring to determine whether the promise made was kept.

How large does a merger have to be before a CA should prevent it? If a merger can significantly reduce costs for the merging companies or otherwise improve their efficiency, should that justify any anticompetitive risks it might create? Merger parties typically claim that the merger is intended to achieve efficiency. Is that even relevant? If so, how? Why is the market power of

---

[2] ACCC v. Pacific National Pty Limited (No. 2) [2019] FCA 669.

*the firm that results from the merger important for competition law anal-
ysis? If the merger has not even occurred yet, how can a CA know enough
about its impact on competition to prevent it? What if a CA learns about a
merger only after it has been completed? What can it do about it? How can a
country seek to avoid that predicament? In our second example, the acquiring
firm made promises about what it would do after the merger. How can competition law "enforce" such promises?*

*Why does the European Commission so extensively investigate the
numerous specific markets at issue and the position of competitors in those
markets? Did the Commission have legal authority to block a merger between two US corporations? If so, why? Should they have (or use) such
authority? See Chapter 11. Many in the US claimed that the Commission
was protecting European companies—that is, engaging in "protectionism."
Why? What relevance, if any, should approval of a merger by one CA have
for a decision on that merger by another CA?*

Combining independent firms into one unit (a merger for competition law purposes) can also harm to competition—sometimes
in many markets in many parts of the world. For example, if
the two largest and most successful manufacturers of computer
chips in the world combine, the consequences will be felt almost everywhere. The resulting entity may have the power to
control prices, exclude competitors, capture for itself technological advances, and prevent new entrants throughout the world.
Combinations involving smaller firms can have similar effects
for a specific country, region, or industry. Where a large foreign
firm acquires local firms in an emerging market this may impede
a country's economic development. As mega-firms acquire other
mega-firms and large firms acquire smaller firms, mergers can re-
shape economies and influence the distribution of wealth in many
societies.

Merger law seeks to prevent mergers that are likely to
have such consequences. This may mean blocking a proposed
merger that the managements of two or more firms have been
negotiating for years, and it often has major consequences for
the companies themselves, their shareholders, their employees,
the economy of one or more countries, or even the shape of an
industry. Not surprisingly, opposition to such "interference" is
often intense.

Most competition laws pursue harmful mergers, but they vary significantly in the way they assess the harms and in the manner and intensity with which they pursue them. Moreover, mergers can have many positive effects, so merger law must make sometimes difficult choices about whether the benefits of a proposed merger outweigh its potential for harm. In doing this, officials apply many of the same principles used for other types of conduct, but they apply them differently, primarily because here they must *predict future harm* rather than *assess past harm*. For some competition law regimes, merger law is a major focus of enforcement; for others it plays a marginal role or none at all. We will see why.

The term "merger law" can be misleading, because its scope is broader than the label suggests. It includes any transaction that results in change of control over a formerly independent firm. This includes not only formal mergers, but also one firm's acquisition of another and joint ventures that have similar effects. This chapter reviews the substantive and procedural principles used in merger law as well as the institutions that apply them and some of the influences on their decisions.

A. MERGER LAW CONTEXTS

Rapidly increasing concentration and globalization of markets and of financial capital have greatly expanded the role and importance of mergers and of merger laws. US antitrust introduced merger controls in the Clayton Act of 1913, but a loophole in the law rendered it largely useless until the loophole was closed in 1952.[3] Prior to the 1990s merger control provisions were almost unknown outside the US. In many jurisdictions, economically significant mergers were few, and the stakes were generally low. Moreover, many governments regulated their territorial markets. As a result, governments had few incentives even to consider a merger law other than in the regulatory framework of specific industries, particularly those related to defense. Since then

---

[3] Celler-Kefauver Act of Dec. 29, 1950, 64 Stat. 1125 (amending the Clayton Antitrust Act of 1914, 38 Stat. 730) (codified at 15 USC §§ 18, 21 (2018)).

economic globalization and its effects have fueled the proliferation of such laws.

For some, these laws are a welcome control on the concentration of economic power and wealth. They provide a legal framework for controlling who merges with whom and thereby protecting the public interest. For others, they represent a subterfuge through which the powerful can manipulate economic developments in the guise of the public interest. Yet others see the provisions as interference with their plans that is likely to limit economic progress and reduce innovation. Merger laws often lead to fierce resistance from business communities. In the EU, for example, such resistance delayed enactment of a merger regulation for roughly twenty-five years—until 1989.[4]

B. KEY FEATURES

Merger law can be highly technical and apparently neutral, but its economic and political importance can also subject it to intense political pressures. It differs from other components of competition law in several important ways.

Administrative focus: Decisions about the legality of a merger need to be made quickly if they are to be effective, so merger law is almost exclusively enforced through administrative institutions. Court procedures are typically too time-consuming. Sometimes judicial review is possible, but in general the role of courts in this area is limited. This creates incentives for firms, lawyers, and economists to focus their attention on influencing CA decisions.

The need to predict: It has to predict the probable consequences of conduct that has not yet occurred, whereas other areas deal primarily with conduct that has already occurred. Its objective is to *prevent* harm to competition rather than to respond to earlier harms.

Technicality: Predicting the effects of a proposed merger is often difficult and uncertain. It invites reliance on those who have the training to make such predictions with some degree of reliability and

---

[4] Council Regulation (EEC) No. 4064/89 [1989] OJ 395 replaced by Council Regulation (EC) No. 139/2004 on the control of concentrations between undertakings (EC Merger Regulation) [2004] OJ L24/1.

whose status can reduce uncertainty, thereby supporting the image that merger control is an objective application of law based on scientific evidence. A result is that economists often play significant roles in merger control, particularly in larger CAs. This use of expertise tends to be costly. Some regimes can afford to hire highly trained economic experts to perform this function, but many cannot.

Global embeddedness: Merger controls are also global in scope. As markets become more global, transnational mergers increase, and merger laws must take these global interrelationships into account. Each CA will be primarily or exclusively concerned with the impact of the merger within its territory and/or on firms based there. This creates incentives for governments to influence CA decisions, but each will also be aware of the potential impact of decisions in other jurisdictions. Dealing with these issues also calls for officials to be well qualified linguistically and technically to effectively present the CA's views in transnational discussions and negotiations.

Merger law features two distinct components: premerger notification and substantive analysis of the probable consequences of a proposed merger.

C. PREMERGER NOTIFICATION

Competition officials need to know about a proposed transaction *before* it is finalized in order to apply merger controls effectively. Once the transaction is completed, it is difficult and often impossible to "unwind" it and return to the status quo. As a result, competition law often requires merging firms to notify the CA of their plans in advance. Failure to notify as required can impair the review process, create delays, and subject the firm to significant fines. Developed competition law regimes typically require notification, but others may have only voluntary notification or none at all. In some regimes (e.g., the EU) premerger notification requirements also establish whether the CA has authority to assess the merger whereas in others (e.g., the US) the substantive jurisdiction of the CA is established separately. This difference is often overlooked, but it can shape the way lawyers approach premerger notification issues.

Triggers: Notification requirements are activated when a merger meets specific thresholds. These typically relate to the size of the firms involved and their sales volume. This filters out mergers that arc not deemed significant enough to warrant a CA's attention. These thresholds are not directly related to whether the merger will have anticompetitive effects, so they can trigger a merger review even where there is little chance of such an effect. For example, they may trigger an investigation (or threat of investigation) in a foreign country in which a relatively insignificant subsidiary of one of the merging parties is located. Mergers in which one or both of the parties are large, multinational companies may have to be notified to thirty or more CAs.[5]

The central issue is typically the definition of markets. The merging firms seek to define the markets as broadly as possible in order to reduce their presumed power in it. Competition officials typically define the market more narrowly. These market definition issues are often the subject of extensive and highly charged discussions between lawyers and economists for the merging firms and competition officials.

Given that a major merger may concern many CAs, differences among them regarding procedures, deadlines, and requested data can be costly and time-consuming. This leads many firms and CAs to call for increased harmonization of the procedures.

D. SUBSTANTIVE REVIEW: PROCEDURES

It is important to distinguish prenotification procedures from substantive merger review. The first merely answers the question of whether the planned merger must be notified; the second asks whether it should be approved, rejected, or modified.

[5] *See* Jacob Bunge and others, 'DuPont, Dow Chemical Agree to Merge, Then Break Up Into Three Companies' (*Wall Street Journal*, December 11, 2015) <https://www. wsj.com/articles/dupont-dow-chemical-agree-to-merge-1449834739?mod=article_inline&mod=article_inline> accessed November 4, 2019; Matthew Schwartz, 'Disney Officially Owns 21st Century Fox' (*NPR*, March 20, 2019) <https://www.npr.org/2019/03/20/705009029/disney-officially-owns-21st-century-fox> accessed November 4, 2019.

Substantive review can use data provided during premerger notification, but the two procedures are fundamentally different, and confusions over the issues involved are common. In general, the merging firms must provide data that enables the CA to evaluate the potential consequences of the merger. This may include information about their products, where they are sold, who their competitors are, what they believe the market to be, what their market shares are, and the like. The digital economy (see Ch. 12) has led to increasing requests for information about the data the firms control.

Merger laws typically authorize a CA to block a merger, at least insofar as the merger affects domestic territory (see Ch. 11) and most CAs have the option of approving a merger subject to the condition that the parties agree to changes proposed by the CA. Basic procedures tend to be similar for most regimes. When a CA receives notification of a planned merger, it has a short period (often thirty days) to notify the parties if it wishes to examine the merger. If it decides not to pursue the investigation, the merger can proceed. Where the CA is not satisfied with the initial investigation, it has one or more periods during which it can examine the merger more closely. During this period it may ask for additional information from the parties as well as explanations of material presented.

These procedures take varied shapes in practice. In regimes such as the US, the EU, Japan, and China, negotiations involving a major merger are often technical, time-consuming, and costly. Economists often play key roles in assessing the likely economic consequences of the merger, and disputes about interpreting data are frequent. The process sometimes receives extensive media attention, and it can also induce political figures to try to influence outcomes. In smaller jurisdictions, the procedures may be far less burdensome and contentious. These CAs often have relatively small staffs with limited resources. They rarely engage in highly sophisticated economic analysis, relying instead on assumptions that make their task manageable. Moreover, they seldom have the political or economic leverage to block a merger outright, although a CA can sometimes require changes intended to reduce the merger's impact within its territory.

E. SUBSTANTIVE
REVIEW: STANDARDS

Statutes typically contain a list of factors that a CA is to take into consideration in evaluating proposed mergers. Together, they are expected to guide the CA in determining the likely harm of the merger. In general, the same principles are used for all types of mergers, but they may be used in differing ways. Horizontal mergers are those between competitors; vertical mergers include mergers between firms that are related vertically (in different markets); all others fall into the category of conglomerate mergers.

Market definition is often a key issue, because it is central to determining the capacity of the merged firm to harm competition. In the last chapter we reviewed market definition in the context of exclusionary conduct. The basic principles are the same in merger law—with one major difference. In merger law, they are applied to *predicting* what the effect will be in the future rather than to analyzing what has happened in the past. This task is obviously more speculative, particularly in fast-changing digital markets.

1. HORIZONTAL MERGERS

A merger of competitors poses particularly significant risks for competition law, so enforcement often focuses on them. By joining two or more competitors into one unit, a horizontal merger necessarily increases concentration in the market(s), and it is this increase in concentration that can harm competition. The main issues are therefore whether the increase is significant enough to cause harm and whether any harmful effects are outweighed by the merger's benefits. If the CA predicts harm, the merging parties typically argue that the concentration levels produced by the merger would not be large enough to cause harm and that the merger will reduce costs and generate efficiencies by, for example, reducing redundancies in personnel or equipment. The focus on prediction creates incentives to hire highly skilled economists who also enjoy particularly high status within the competition law community. Regardless of sophistication levels, however, predictions must be based on assumptions about the future, and the potential for conflict is ever present.

Concentration levels are measured in several ways. For example, some use fairly straightforward formulae such as whether the merger will significantly increase the market share of the leading firms (often the top four) with the largest market shares. A more sophisticated analysis is likely to use the so-called Herfindahl-Hirshman index, which applies a mathematical formula to the array of market shares in the market both before and after the merger. This produces a single number that represents the increase in the concentration level and signals the likelihood that the merger may cause harm.

Once changes in concentration levels have been identified, the CA must evaluate the merger's effects on competition law's goals. Most merger analysis focuses entirely or primarily on a merger's economic effects, specifically whether it creates or strengthens market power in the post-merger firm. The creation or strengthening of market power is typically considered the key determinant of competitive harm. In digital markets, the control of data is increasingly taken into account as a source of power. Some merger regimes also consider political and social factors in evaluating the effects of the merger.

Regimes differ in their assessment of probable harm from mergers and in their evaluation of potential justifications for them. For example, regimes that rely on economic analysis may be more receptive to arguments that the merger's potential contributions to competition in the future, whereas those that are particularly sensitive to the effects of power on economic freedom or on protection of domestic industries may give less weight to these factors.

2. VERTICAL MERGERS

Vertical mergers are more complicated, because they do not directly eliminate competition among competitors. They can, however, have anticompetitive effects through their impact on related markets. Many of the issues here are similar to those we encountered in the context of vertical agreements, so we will not review those in detail here. The primary concern in most regimes is the potential for vertical mergers to foreclose competition in affected markets. Where a firm acquires a supplier of raw materials to its market, for example, it may be in a position to reduce the supply of the product to its rivals and thereby put them at a competitive disadvantage. This is similar to concerns in vertical agreements, but a merger is more permanent than an agreement and therefore poses greater risks.

There are important differences among regimes in their evaluation of vertical mergers. Where a regime bases the analysis on identifiable and quantifiable economic effects alone, it is less likely to intervene in vertical mergers, because proving their effects is often difficult and somewhat speculative. On the other hand, where a CA is not subject to these strict standards of evaluation, it has greater flexibility to consider other factors in evaluating the merger. For example, it may pay particular attention to its effects on the country's economic development and therefore see greater potential for harm from the merger.

Where a foreign firm from a capital-exporting country acquires a domestic firm in an emerging market, the domestic CA is likely to pay particular attention to it. In many emerging market countries, there is significant controversy about the effects of such vertical integration. Many fear that foreign control is likely to hamper economic development. Others see it as a welcome infusion of capital. Lawyers and economists need to be aware of these concerns.

3. CONGLOMERATE MERGERS

Mergers in which the parties are neither in competition with each other nor in a vertical relationship have no direct effects on competition, so there is limited enforcement regarding these mergers. Some jurisdictions do pay attention, however, to the potential for "deep pocket" effects. The central idea here is that where a large firm acquires greater resources, this may discourage other firms from entering the market and discipline rivals already in it. As with vertical mergers, this is often a particularly sensitive issue in emerging markets.

F. GLOBAL PATTERNS
AND DYNAMICS

Merger control plays a particularly prominent role in the global system for three main reasons. First, transborder mergers inevitably call for direct contact among CAs. A major transaction may be reviewed by numerous authorities—potentially involving each of the countries that might be affected by it, and decisions in one will often affect the interests of one or more of the others. Officials may be in contact with each other to coordinate investigations, clarify factual material, and predict what others will do or seek support for their positions on the merger. Those who accept the merger may, for example, try to influence others to do the same or simply try to predict what others will do. This creates fields of interaction in which power, influence, and negotiating skill are put in play. The resulting decisions often have major consequences for the businesses involved and sometimes for national political and economic interests.

A second factor is that merger regimes are particularly vulnerable to outside pressures—both financial and political. This introduces an additional dynamic into the negotiations that can cause suspicion and tension. If, for example, one competition authority (e.g., the Japanese Fair Trade Commission) is subject to little or no external influence, the Japanese officials are likely to be frustrated in dealing with another CA that is apparently influenced by factors other than law.

The economic and social importance of many mergers often highlights blind spots in the views of officials with different backgrounds. For example, an official from a rich, high technology country may have no experience with the concerns of an official from a small, less industrial country—and vice versa. These differences in experience often shape the interpretation of data.

Finally, differences and similarities among regimes inevitably play a significant role in these interactions, so all are aware of the potential value of reducing them. Recommendations by the International Competition Network and other transnational organizations have led to greater similarity among states regarding, for example, procedural issues such as the information required for premerger notification and the time periods to be used in merger review. This saves costs for the firms involved and tends to facilitate communication and coordination among CAs, so there is widespread support for it.

There is much less standardization regarding the substantive principles to be applied in assessing mergers, and they often harbor significant potential for misunderstanding, tension, and conflict. One factor is a sharp difference in the concepts used. Some regimes, for example, the US, rely on a "lessening of competition" standard, which focuses on identifying the economic effects of the merger. Other regimes use a European-style "dominance" standard. Here the analysis asks whether the merger would create or strengthen a dominant position, and it often includes an assessment of both economic effects and other factors such as economic freedom. The language and concepts differ, and they can lead to different results, but often the results are similar. Some regimes (e.g., the EU) combine the two standards.

The differing standards are associated with different patterns of enforcement. Regimes that rely on standard economic analysis tend to focus on horizontal mergers and consider vertical mergers generally less harmful. Others that consider longer term effects or social and political factors may pay more attention to vertical mergers. Regimes in which development concerns are prominent often pay particular attention to acquisitions of domestic firms by foreign firms and on acquisitions that may have political and social consequences.

Regimes assess mergers with vastly different resources and often therefore quite different tools. This necessarily impedes communication among officials. If, for example, a PhD-level economist in the EU analyzes the merger from an econometric perspective and wants to discuss the assessment with an official with little or no training in econometrics, the EU official may not only have difficulty explaining the basis for the assessment, but s/he will also be inclined to believe that his/her expertise is more valuable and more defensible than opinions from those with less training and fewer tools.

G. COMMENT

The concentration of control over economic resources heightens concern about mergers, particularly when they also influence other social issues such as privacy. Tech giants have become a major cause of concern. Merger control has grown rapidly in importance since the 1990s in response to these threats, creating increasingly strong incentives to try to influence decisions in this area of law. Understanding the dynamics of merger review and predicting outcomes can be challenging, but it creates opportunities for those who can deal with it most effectively.

PART III

INDIVIDUAL COMPETITION LAWS: MODELS, PATTERNS, AND KEYS

National (and sometimes regional—e.g., EU) institutions enact and enforce competition law. They make the decisions that shape markets, and they are the main actors in the global system, so this part of the Guide looks at what they do, how they do it, and factors that drive and mold their decisions. Each regime pursues its own goals and uses its own methods and procedures, but there are also significant similarities among them. In this Part of the Guide we bring these regimes into focus—to help make sense of information about them, recognize what is important to know in each, locate them in the global competition law system, and highlight differences and similarities among them.

Two regimes are so central to competition law that each has its own chapter—the US (Ch. 8) and the EU (Ch. 9). Both are of major practical importance for lawyers and businesses; each also influences others in important ways; and they play central roles in the global system. We need insight into them in order to grasp competition law's dimensions and dynamics.

Other regimes (Ch. 10) do not play this kind of central role, so the Guide deals with them differently: it identifies the factors that shape them. These factors provide guideposts to what is important to know about any regime. They enable us to recognize the dynamics of the regime itself and to see similarities and differences among regimes. Some factors shape *"families"* of regimes, so recognizing them can provide valuable insights into similarities and differences within these groupings and relationships within them. Chapter 10 identifies factors that are key in each of these contexts.

8

US ANTITRUST LAW: CENTRAL, BUT UNIQUE

US antitrust law has long been at or near the center of the competition law world, and it continues to influence all who deal with this branch of law. For some, it is a model to be followed, because it offers solutions to problems they face. Others seek to learn from US experience and the rich and varied writing about it. Still others see it as an "international standard" that they must pursue. The size of the US market, the political weight of the US, and the expertise of its scholars and officials make it important for many non-US lawyers, officials, and business leaders. It also influences competition law regimes throughout the global arena. Curiously, it is also highly unique—quite an irony.

A. SHAPING US ANTITRUST

Three background factors are particularly helpful for understanding US antitrust law (the references in this chapter are to federal-level antitrust law). First, it has evolved within a society where competition itself is a powerful cultural value. Unlike most other competition laws, it has not had to create a "competition culture." Second, the US is a large and politically powerful country with a vast and technologically advanced market that has evolved around and through the mechanism of competition. And third, its institutions and representatives have aggressively promoted US-style competition law to the rest of the world for decades, even though the content of US law has changed dramatically.

Decisions made in creating antitrust law in 1890 set in place central features of the regime that have shaped and controlled its evolution since then. The US Congress enacted the Sherman Act—the initial (and still basic) antitrust statute—in response to

Competition Law and Antitrust. David J. Gerber, Oxford University Press (2020). © David J. Gerber.
DOI: 10.1093/oso/9780198727477.001.0001

populist political pressure to control giant corporations (then known as "trusts").[1] The idea of a general law to combat anticompetitive conduct was virtually unknown, so the legislators had no models. A few very basic statutes had been created in states of the US during the previous few years, but they had not functioned in any significant way, and no national government had created such a legal regime.

The Congress found a simple solution in which they made two concepts—"restraint of trade" and "monopolization"—enforceable in the federal courts that had previously been used for other purposes in other contexts. The statute's language is exceptionally sparse and general. In essence, it leaves to the courts the entire responsibility for creating and controlling the substantive content of the law. In 1913 the Clayton Act added a few new elements for special situations (e.g., mergers).[2] These two statutes have served as the basic texts of US antitrust law ever since.

The decision to make the federal courts responsible for developing antitrust law has led to a regime that relies on decisions by judges in individual cases. Not surprisingly, this has not generated a well-ordered legal framework that can be readily understood. Case decisions vary significantly in both their reasoning and their conclusions. There are also very many cases, and sometimes they are long, unclear, and inconsistent. Antitrust specialists generally know how to operate in this dense and apparently disorderly system, but outsiders typically do not have the knowledge necessary to do so. This often leaves them with vague images of the US regime and tempts them to notice and emphasize those elements that suit their objectives.

B. GOALS

Antitrust goals must be gleaned from judicial opinions, but the goals have varied significantly over time, and the changes are often difficult to recognize, especially for outside viewers. Prior

---

[1] Sherman Antitrust Act, ch. 647, 26 Stat. 209 (codified as amended at 15 USC §§ 1–7 (2018)).

[2] Clayton Antitrust Act, 38 Stat. 730 (codified as amended at 15 USC §§ 12–27 (2018); 29 USC §§ 52–53 (2018)).

to the 1970s the courts were primarily concerned with the domestic impact of antitrust law, often focusing on issues such as
fairness (particularly for small and medium-sized firms), economic liberty, and equality of opportunity among competitors.
The "Law and Economics Revolution" changed this dramatically beginning in the 1970s. With encouragement from academic
writers and supported by the perceived need to reduce burdens on
US businesses, the courts have significantly narrowed the goals to
the point where they are almost exclusively economic, focusing
on the efficiency of the economy and benefits to consumers.

This fundamental change in goals can make decisions particularly difficult to understand. Judicial opinions that were based
on earlier goals are often still cited for a variety of purposes, even
though the goals they served have changed. This typically happens
where a court wants to support its decision by appealing to the
precedential value of general principles stated in an earlier case
even where it may not follow the reasoning of the case opinion.
An insider may learn to recognize this mixture of references, but
it often baffles external viewers.

The broader goals that once animated US antitrust law have all
but disappeared from judicial opinions, but not from American
society. Some voices continue to call for bringing at least some of
them back into the picture.

C. METHODS AND
SUBSTANTIVE LAW

The economic goals of consumer welfare and efficiency fore-
ground economic methods, but judges are not economists, and
they make the decisions about what the law is. This produces an
interplay of economic and legal methods, as the methods of economics are filtered through the legal language and case-based
methods of lawyers and judges. Institutions and their procedures
mold the interplay.

Because antitrust statutes do not provide clear guidance
to courts, judges are required to base their decisions on prior
cases that the US legal system designates as "binding" on them.
Competition Authorities (CAs) must also treat cases as authoritative, not only formally, but also because the courts that review

CA decisions consider them binding. This case-based reasoning calls for courts to compare the facts and reasoning of relevant prior decisions with the facts and reasoning of the case before them. The task is inevitably somewhat subjective—which facts are relevant? How does the reasoning of the earlier cases apply to the new case? The factual density of many antitrust cases further increases discretion in making this comparison. This makes decisions opaque for many viewers. In contrast, economic methods are abstract, universal, and primarily based on the assumption that actors act rationally (with some variations—see Ch. 3). Highly trained and expensive competition economists may use formal models in applying them. A court in an antitrust case must integrate information, assumptions, and predictions from often highly complex economic models into a dense context of cases while giving priority to the current economics-based goals. We will see that US court procedures make this task both easier and more difficult than it might seem.

D. INSTITUTIONS AND PROCEDURES

Understanding the institutional vocabulary of the regime gives us insight into how it generates decisions. It is a unique mixture of courts and administrative institutions that has remained largely unchanged for many decades.

1. THE COMPETITION AUTHORITIES: THE DOJ AND THE FTC

Two separate federal authorities are responsible for public enforcement. Both are located in Washington, DC. They typically agree on a division of responsibilities between them, but sometimes their agreements are neither "official" nor well known, so it is necessary to ask an "insider" about which institution is likely to handle a specific case. They sometimes compete with each other for control of particular types of conduct or merely for status.

One is the US Justice Department (DoJ), which is part of the executive branch of government and subject, therefore, to political control. In general, it cannot enforce antitrust law by it-self, but must win a lawsuit to do so. It may sue for either civil or criminal remedies, depending on the gravity of the conduct and other factors such as the intent of the defendants.

The other is the Federal Trade Commission (FTC). It can en-force the law directly through fines and other orders, but its or-ders are reviewable by the regular courts, so it must also follow the principles established by the courts. It is an independent agency, so it is less easily influenced by the political system than the DoJ, but it depends on Congress for funding, so in practice it must sometimes deal with political influence.

Many higher-level administrators (especially in the DoJ) prac-tice competition law before going into government and return to their legal practices after leaving their public posts. Where this occurs, they seldom remain in their positions for long periods. As a result, the interests, perspectives, and values of practitioners often play central roles in these institutions. In contrast, for ex-ample, officials of the German Federal Cartel Office or Japanese Fair Trade Commission typically spend their entire careers in that office, amass extensive experience there, and enjoy a high degree of protection from outside pressures.

2. COURTS

The federal courts are general jurisdiction courts that handle many types of cases, which means that the judges do not specialize in specific types of cases. They are appointed by the President for life, typically after decades of experience in private practice. As a group, they enjoy high social status and have a high reputation for independence. Corruption is rare. This generates confidence within the antitrust community that antitrust law is protected from outside pressures, and, in turn, this leads many to believe that the independence of competition law requires a central role for courts. The courts play central roles in both public and pri-vate antitrust enforcement, and they employ basically the same procedures in both contexts.

Procedures in US antitrust litigation are extremely important in shaping the law. Their underlying principles also differ sig-nificantly from most other procedural systems, so they are often misunderstood. Unlike many other competition law regimes, the procedures are not specifically adapted to the needs of antitrust law. With few exceptions, the courts use these general procedures in antitrust cases. If the DoJ sues to enforce the law, it can seek criminal prosecution under criminal procedure, civil procedure for fines, or other remedies. The FTC's actions can be reviewed according to the standards and procedures for review of administrative actions.

Three general procedural traits are particularly significant for understanding US antitrust and relating it to other regimes. First, attorneys for the parties perform many tasks that judges typically perform in other legal systems. Each is given authority to acquire relevant factual material and shape a factual story that is then presented to the court. Each side presents its own story. This differs from most jurisdictions, where the judge is primarily responsible for acquiring data and constructing his/her own factual story. Where there is a jury (yes, there can be a jury in civil antitrust litigation) it makes the final decision regarding facts (subject to some control by the judge) and the judge makes decisions concerning law. If there is no jury, the judge makes the decisions on both fact and law. Second, the procedure is heavily fact-oriented. This focus on facts deserves emphasis, because it promotes legal doctrines that tend to be nuanced and to depend for their persuasiveness on detailed factual analysis. It also tends to generate complex and expensive litigation. This contrasts sharply with procedures in most other countries, where often only a court can demand information and only to the extent that it is directly related to the statutory requirements for a specific competition law claim. Third, where a court serves as an appeal body, the review is generally limited to questions of law. In many regimes, reviewing courts may also review lower court conclusions about the facts in the case.

3. PRIVATE ENFORCEMENT

Most US antitrust cases are based on private enforcement. Cases are initiated and pursued according to private calculations of benefit and cost, not concern for the law's consistency or for government economic policy. Foreign observers frequently fail to recognize the importance of such litigation in the US antitrust regime. Moreover, private enforcement is direct rather than secondary ("piggy-back") as it is in most other jurisdictions in which private enforcement is allowed. Potential plaintiffs need not await the action of a CA or other government agency before pursuing their private claims. Moreover, the procedural obstacles that restrict the use of private enforcement in other systems are generally absent.

One central feature of private enforcement deserves special note, primarily because it influences the shape, procedure, legal doctrine, and costs of private litigation. This is the so-called "discovery" procedure, according to which each party in a court case is entitled to request and receive a broad range of potentially relevant information from its opponent that it can use in the litigation and present to the court. This procedure can be expensive and time-consuming, and it generally means that extensive data is provided to the decision-maker (judge or jury) and that the factual basis for claims can be extensively contested. The often vast amounts of data tend to shape not only individual litigation, but also the substance of antitrust law.

The law also provides incentives for private litigation, and the legal profession makes full use of them. For example, the law provides triple compensation for violations—that is, the actual compensation is trebled—as well as punitive compensation. Other features of the system further encourage lawyers to pursue private litigation. Contingent fees (*pacta de quota litis*) are common, and US antitrust lawyers are known for aggressive pursuit of private cases. Moreover, high-cost private litigation is common and culturally approved in the US, so business leaders are accustomed to its high costs.

E. THE DYNAMICS OF ANTITRUST

The interplay of economists and lawyers is the central dynamic of the US regime. Economists have become almost indispensable in litigation. They influence the content of the law, because the goals of antitrust law are conceived primarily in economic terms. Many economists now specialize in antitrust issues. Some are members of university faculties, but the increased importance of economics in antitrust has also generated specialized consulting firms that employ significant numbers of specialized economists on a full-time basis.

Legal practitioners interact with economists to translate economic knowledge and views into legal claims and arguments. They present arguments to administrative and judicial decision-makers, manage litigation, and advise clients, but they rely on economists to identify, assess, and interpret information that is economically relevant. They work with economists to construct arguments that are consistent with the economic criteria established in the economics literature and in prior cases. Judges are trained as lawyers, and almost all have been practitioners. As a result, practitioners and judges share common educational and professional experiences, speak the same conceptual language, and maintain personal relationships based on those experiences. Legal scholars are sometimes influential in shaping this lawyer–economist relationship.

F. TARGETS

A brief look at antitrust's targets is important for two main reasons. First, the worldwide reach of US law and the size of the US market make the information practically valuable for many lawyers and their clients. Second, US experience is widely referred to (and often misunderstood) by those making competition law decisions in other regimes.

1. AGREEMENTS

US law dealing with agreements is important for understanding discussions of the subject within the US regime, but it also plays a role globally. Section 1 of the Sherman Act prohibits agreements "in restraint of trade," but, as noted above, the statute does not define the term, so the courts have had to give meaning to it. They developed two central concepts that are often used (sometimes mistakenly) in other regimes. One is "rule of reason." This concept was developed by the courts to give more specific meaning to "restraint of trade." In general, it refers in US usage

to weighing the harm to competition from an agreement against
its benefits to competition, although the myriad court opinions
that have interpreted this language have attached related concepts
that modify this general claim. The most important of these is
the concept of "ancillary restraint," which provides that an agreement that serves only to support another (legitimate) agreement
may satisfy rule of reason requirements. The term "rule of reason"
is often used much more loosely in other regimes—for example,
to refer to a deviation from a statutory rule or to a "reasonable"
application of the law. The author has heard uses in other regimes
that would make little sense in US discussions.

The second key term is "per se" violation. The courts developed it to designate specific types of conduct that are *inherently*
unreasonable. It rests on the idea that the courts have accumulated
enough experience with a particular kind of conduct to be confident that it is anticompetitive. Where a violation is labeled "per
se," a plaintiff need only prove that the conduct occurred in order
to prevail in litigation. There is no need for a rule of reason analysis. This reduces the costs of litigation for plaintiffs and increases
the likelihood of success. It is generally far easier and less expensive to prove that conduct fits within a designated category than
to establish a preponderance of anticompetitive effects through a
rule of reason investigation. These terms are part of the analysis
of both horizontal and vertical agreements.

Horizontal agreements: Cartels are the main target of US antitrust as they have been through much of its evolution. Judicial
decisions dealing with them number in the thousands. Prior to
the law and economics revolution, this was largely because an
agreement by competitors to reduce competition among them
seemed an obvious restriction of competition. The cases centered
on issues such as what constituted an agreement and whether the
political or other benefits produced by the agreement outweighed
its harm to competition. The shift of antitrust's goals to economic
effects maintained this importance, but changed the reasoning. In
this view, the key factor is whether the agreements are economically harmful. Moreover, as we saw in Chapter 5, economists can
be far more confident in identifying harm from cartel agreements
than when analyzing other forms of conduct.

The scope and expense of employing a full rule of reason analysis has led courts to shorten the analysis for some categories of cases. One is a so-called "la look" procedure that employs a variety of criteria to determine whether an agreement should be given a fuller analysis. Another is to give judges extensive discretion to limit the extent of the fact-finding ("discovery") procedure.

Vertical agreements: Before the economics-based changes in the goals of antitrust many types of vertical agreements were considered per se violations, but economists have demonstrated the potential hazards of applying per se analysis to them. The effects of a vertical agreement depend on many factors (see Ch. 5) so there is a significant risk that per se treatment will result in prohibiting agreements that are not actually harmful to competition. This has led courts to eliminate per se status from almost all vertical agreements and, therefore, to a dramatic decline in enforcement against them. It makes outcomes more difficult to predict and litigation far more costly. The need to analyze the effects of conduct calls for extensive data collection in two or more markets, which makes the process potentially very expensive.

Unilateral conduct: monopolization: As we have seen, section 2 of the Sherman Act uses the concept of "monopolization@" to identify single-firm conduct that harms competition. The term itself is unclear, and more than a century of experience has done little to give it a clearer meaning. The use of a more effects-based analysis has further diminished its utility. Courts have identified several forms of monopolization, for example, predatory pricing, refusals to deal, and use of intellectual property rights to prevent or impede competition, but proving that specific conduct has led to specific effects has often proven elusive.

Mergers and acquisitions: The impact of economics-based analysis (also known as effects-based analysis) on agreements extends to the merger context: a greater focus on horizontal mergers and relatively little attention to other areas.

G. STATE ANTITRUST LAWS

Each of the states of the US has its own antitrust laws. All are basically similar to the federal law, although they are often significantly more detailed, and there are some significant differences in the details. They are seldom applied to conduct on national and international markets, so they are of limited importance for most antitrust practitioners and foreign observers. In general, they are also weakly enforced. Nevertheless, a few (e.g., New York state antitrust law) occasionally play a role in these contexts, so advising about specific conduct requires checking for potential state antitrust law issues.

H. THE US IN THE GLOBAL ANTITRUST SYSTEM

As noted at the beginning of this chapter, US antitrust law plays many key roles in the global system—point of reference, source of experience, expertise and support, potential international standard, and powerful agent for promoting an effects-based approach to competition law.

These roles and images encourage US representatives to play an aggressive role in the global system. Most of them view the basic principles and approaches of US antitrust law with satisfaction— or at least as preferable to its alternatives. Few would consider them unblemished, but most consider them to be basically "right." As a result, they often seek to convince others to emulate them. The unique evolution of the US regime and its relations with other competition law systems combine to shape these US attitudes.

US economic and political power also supports the global influence of US antitrust law. The political weight of the US government has at times been used to influence the development of foreign systems. Moreover, the government has sometimes used aid and technical assistance programs to induce foreign jurisdictions to conform competition law decisions to the wishes of the US.

Private power and influence play less obvious, but nevertheless important roles. For example, US officials and lawyers often play leading roles in international organizations and meetings. Their prominence and influence are based on many factors, including their experience in international competition law matters, particularly in the use of economics, the richness of US scholarship, and the practical importance of US antitrust enforcement throughout the world. US lawyers and economists also benefit from the influence of the business firms, law firms, and other private institutions with which they are associated. These firms often commit significant resources to influencing foreign decision-makers to favor the interests of their clients. This creates incentives for their counterparts in other countries to seek contacts with them for their own benefit—for example, through the potential for client referrals. Finally, the image that US law represents the "right way" to do competition law gives members of the US antitrust community something to sell that can have benefits for them. Where others follow the US, they typically turn to US professionals for guidance and advice.

★★★

US antitrust law and experience have long been at the center of discussions about competition law, and this has given it influence in many foreign regimes. Some support this central role, but others are not so sure.

9

COMPETITION LAW IN EUROPE

European competition law is the other central player in the competition law world. Virtually all firms operating beyond their own
national boundaries need to pay attention to it, many regimes use
it as a model and reference point, and its institutions have broad
and often deep influence on many others. Some aspects of the
substantive law are similar to US antitrust, but the similarities
are sometimes misleading, and its methods, institutions, and
procedures often differ greatly from their US counterparts.

National and EU institutions function together to create,
apply, and enforce competition law in Europe. In this chapter we
look at this integrated regime, some of the main substantive principles it has developed, key factors that shape decisions within it,
and its role in the global system. The regime is complex, so the
chapter is arranged to cut through its complexity. It begins with
an overview of the basic architecture in order to provide a sense
of the whole. It then clarifies the roles of member states in the
system; inspects the EU's institutions, methods, and substantive
law; and shows how the EU institutions interact with national
systems to generate decisions.

A. THE BASIC ARCHITECTURE

The European system interweaves national and EU institutions and
roles. EU institutions—primarily the European Commission—
create and develop the policies and principles of competition
law for the entire EU. They also steer application of the law
by the member states, although member state institutions vary
in their willingness to follow the guidance of EU institutions.
Member states are the primary enforcers of EU law, which they
are required to apply to most transactions, but in some cases the
Commission itself enforces the law, and in some member states

Competition Law and Antitrust. David J. Gerber, Oxford University Press (2020). © David J. Gerber.
DOI: 10.1093/oso/9780198727477.001.0001

the Commission informally directs the state's application of the law. Each member also has its own competition law. These typically become relevant only when conduct has consequences that are confined within the state's borders. If the consequences extend beyond the state's boundaries, it must apply EU law, so it seldom has incentives to apply its own law to the same conduct.

B. MEMBER STATE ROLES

Member states play two main roles in the system: they provide the ideas and experiences that inform its substantive and procedural principles, and they enforce EU law through their own institutions and procedures. These institutions have their own interests and incentives, which do not always align with those of EU institutions, and recognizing this can be of much value in predicting enforcement decisions.

1. MEMBER STATE EXPERIENCE

A brief look at the evolution of competition law in Europe provides insights into the regime's principles and institutions. Throughout this development, leaders saw competition law as a response to economic and social problems such as industrialization, economic inequality, postwar reconstruction and inflation. Several of the driving ideas were first articulated in the 1890s in Vienna, the capital of the Habsburg Empire, where the drafters viewed them as a tool for improving Austria's economic performance (and catching up with Germany). From there they spread to Germany and to other parts of Europe. By the late 1920s competition law had become an important issue of economic policy in Europe, and a basic consensus about it had begun to take shape.

Two ideas dominate the model that evolved there. First, competition law's main goal should be to control private economic power, because that power could be used to distort the competitive process and undermine its potential value. Second, administrators rather than courts should exercise this control because they were in the best position to wield the state's power against powerful firms. Courts were not considered appropriate for the task. These principles became deeply embedded in thinking about competition law and continue to have influence.

Competition laws were weakly enforced, if at all, for decades. European states had far weightier issues on their agendas—depressions and wars, for example. Statutes were vague, administrative decisions were seldom free from politics, and they could only be reviewed by administrative courts for violation of procedural principles.

This began to change in the late 1950s, first in Germany and eventually in many other European states. German support for a competition law was a response to its disastrous experiences during the first half of the century and the belief by many that excessive concentration of economic power had facilitated the Nazi takeover. One group of lawyers and economists known as "ordoliberals" (roughly, "freedom within order") believed that laws were needed to protect the competitive process from interference from *both the state and private enterprise*. They believed that competition law could be a means of achieving that goal, but only if it was conceived as "law" and decisions were produced by relatively independent institutions, using *judicial* methods and legal procedures. In this view, it could not be effective if it was merely "policy" made primarily by administrative officials and easily changed and subverted.

The ordoliberals were passionately committed to this objective, and when they gained important positions in postwar Germany, they pushed to enact the German Law against Restraints of Competition (GWB) in 1957—the first "modern" competition law in Europe.[1] In it, an independent authority would apply competition law, and its decisions could be appealed on *both* procedure and substance to the *regular courts* and thus to *judicial reasoning and constraints*. This law was enforced with vigor and commitment, and many saw it as an important factor in the success of the German social market economy.

Over the following decades other European states introduced new competition laws and inserted more "law-based" elements

---

[1] Germany's Act Against Restraints of Competition, Law of July 27, 1957, as amended 1965, 1973, 1976, 1980, 1989, 1998, 2005, 2013, and 2017.

into existing ones. They increasingly protected decision-makers from external political and economic influences, relied on juridical methods and procedures, emphasized the need for consistent treatment of similar fact patterns, made the decision-making process more transparent, and enhanced the capacity of Competition Authorities (CAs) to investigate and impose sanctions on violators.

These national experiences shaped competition law as it took shape in the institutions of the EU after its creation in 1957.[2] They contributed ideas, values, and experiences that were adopted and adapted to the needs of European integration. At times US antitrust law experience also played a role in this evolution.

2. MEMBER STATES AS THE PRIMARY ENFORCERS OF EU COMPETITION LAW

In 2004, the relationship between the member states and the EU changed abruptly, primarily in response to an increase in the number of member states.[3] In the new arrangement, member state CAs became the primary enforcers of EU law for most purposes. They were now required to apply EU competition law to conduct that had consequences beyond their own borders. This meant that they had to apply EU law to virtually all major transactions. As a consequence, the member states have basically aligned their domestic competition laws with EU law. It is important to emphasize, however, that states sometimes vary in their interpretations of the law.

The EU Commission "steers" member state enforcement. It monitors the decisions of the CAs in order to assure that the law is being interpreted consistently across the EU. A decision by a CA that deviates too far from EU principles and policies can be expected to lead EU officials to request that it be brought into line. The European Competition Network (ECN)—an organization of CAs—has the same basic objective.[4] It sponsors dialogue and

---

[2] Treaty Establishing the European Economic Community (Rome Treaty) [1957].

[3] Council Regulation (EC) No. 1/2003 on the implementation of the rules of competition laid down in Articles 81 and 82 of the Treaty [2003] OJ L1/1 amended by Regulation (EC) No. 411/2004 [2004] OJ L68.

[4] European Commission, 'Overview—European Competition Network' (*European Commission*) <https://ec.europa.eu/competition/ecn/index_en.html> accessed November 4, 2019.

cooperation among CAs with the aim of generating greater uniformity and effectiveness within the EU. Without these forms of control, enforcement could diverge and undermine integration.

EU authorities have much less influence on member state courts. Their decisions are therefore more likely to diverge significantly from EU guidelines, so it is necessary to check both administrative and court decisions when assessing the legal situation in a member state.

C. EU INSTITUTIONS: ACTORS AND VOICES

Recognizing what EU institutions do, how they do it, and what incentives they have is a key to interpreting and predicting EU decisions.

1. THE COMMISSION AND ITS ROLES

The EU Commission (the "Commission") is the EU's central bureaucracy and the focal point of EU competition law. Its officials are obligated to foster the interests of the EU as a whole and not to represent national interests. In competition law, they are generally protected from direct external political influences.

Competition law issues are handled by the Directorate General for Competition (DG Comp) which has three main responsibilities. One is to create and develop policy. It drafts guidelines and policy statements regarding its views and practices. A second is to apply competition law in specific situations that are reserved for enforcement at the EU level. The third is to guide member state enforcement. The Director General of this office directs its operations and often plays an important role in shaping policy and relations with other components of the bureaucracy.

The Commissioner for Competition is responsible to the full Commission for the handling of competition issues. Her influence on the DG is often extensive, because she must agree to its recommendations before presenting them to the Commission for decision. Major decisions must be approved by the full Commission, but in practice and by necessity it typically endorses the DG's recommendations. As a result, the Commissioner is typically a center of attraction for the media and the principal spokesperson for EU competition law.

The Office of Legal Services is a component of the Commission that often plays an important role in competition law. It reviews proposed decisions of DG Comp for conformity with EU treaties and laws. If it considers a proposed DG decision a violation, it negotiates with the DG for changes, and it can compel changes in the proposed decisions.

2. EU COURTS AND THE EUROPEAN PARLIAMENT

The two EU courts develop principles and rules in the context of reviewing enforcement decisions of the Commission, and firms that have been fined by the Commission bring most cases. The General Court (previously, the Court of First Instance) handles most competition cases. Its decisions can sometimes be appealed to the European Court of Justice although for practical reasons this is not common. The judges on the two courts are proposed by their respective member states, and they are typically approved by consensus after negotiation among EU members.

The European Parliament typically plays a marginal role in competition law. The Commission must, however, report its activities to the Parliament, and members of the Parliament have opportunities to question Commission decisions and to publicize what they consider its errors and weaknesses. Parliament debates can provide useful insights into the factors that are influencing Commission decisions.

D. GOALS

EU competition law pursues a mix of goals, at times emphasizing one goal or group of goals, while at other times pursuing others. Two have been central throughout the evolution of the competition law regime. Each has changed shape over time, and the two have gradually merged into one interrelated and not always easily predictable set of goals.

One theme has been to support European integration. This was central to the EU during its formative period. The success of European integration was uncertain for decades after the creation of the EU, and competition law was frequently used as a tool to break down private borders to trade between the member states and focus attention on the benefits of a larger, more unified European market. For example, in one important early case, competition law was applied to invalidate the private use of intellectual property rights to segment the EU market into national markets. One component of this integration theme was the belief that if competition provided benefits to broad segments of population, they would be more likely to support continuing integration. This use of competition law was generally seen as effective, and it was a focus of competition law efforts until the 1990s.

The other central goal has been to protect the competitive process from harm—that is, to make markets more effective. Conceptions of harm have evolved over time, but a continuing thread has been concern about the use of economic power to "distort" competition. This is a generic goal of competition law that is not necessarily related to the integration process.

These two basic goals began to merge in the 1990s, when developments in US antitrust law were seen as contributing to the successes of the US economy. This nudged decision-makers toward a "more economic approach"—that is, greater attention to efficiency and consumer welfare. EU officials have seen this economics-based approach as itself contributing to European integration by providing a common framework for use throughout the EU system. In this view, integration goals are no longer separate from economic goals.

The relationship between economic and integration goals will inevitably continue to evolve, forming an amalgam of goals from which EU decision-makers can draw in making decisions. The result is flexibility and adaptability, but also degrees of uncertainty. In general, however, careful review of recent administrative and judicial decisions reveals the goals that are favored by the Commission and the courts at a particular time, and this can significantly reduce uncertainty.

E. SUBSTANTIVE LAW METHODS AND TARGETS

1. BASIC STRUCTURE

In contrast to the case-based antitrust law of the US, EU substantive law is based primarily on the governing treaty and interpretations of the treaty provisions by the courts and the Commission. The Rome treaty that created the earlier versions of the EU in 1957 contains two basic provisions, and they have been maintained, most recently in the TFEU of 2004.[5] One treats agreements; the other includes abuse of dominance, and there are separate provisions for mergers.

Article 101(1) prohibits agreements that restrain competition either as object or effect. This creates a very broad category of potential violations, but paragraph (3) of the same article creates a set of four exemptions that significantly narrow this category. They are the EU's version of the balancing function described in Chapter 5, but they are more structured than the US version of balancing. In outline, agreements are exempt if they (1) contribute to improving the production or distribution of goods or to technical or economic progress, (2) and allow a fair share of the benefits to go to consumers, (3) do not impose restrictions that are not necessary to attaining those objectives, and (4) do not create the potential for the undertakings to eliminate competition in a relevant market. The reach of these exemptions is typically the focus of competition law attention.

The EU courts have produced an extensive body of judicial decisions which all institutions that apply EU law are expected to follow. Their methods of interpretation combine three main strands. One is the European continental legal tradition, which pays close attention to the process of interpreting fixed legal texts. Most judges have been trained in this "civil law tradition." A second is the unique legal character of the EU and the existentially high value of integration. Finally, there is the need to consider the economic effects of conduct in applying the legal provisions.

---

[5] Treaty on the Functioning of the European Union [2012] OJ L326/47.

The Commission is bound to follow judicial interpretations, but Commission decisions are not always completely consistent with each other over time. Sometimes this is related to differences in the training and experience of officials—some are legally trained, while others are trained in areas such as economics. Nevertheless, the Commission provides numerous guidelines and other information about its current decision practices. In dealing with individual cases, it is necessary to pay close attention to this information, which the Commission makes easily accessible on its website.

2. TARGETS

Horizontal agreements: The perceived importance of identifying economic harm leads to a focus on horizontal agreements. Economics plays a central role in assessing these agreements, but, in contrast to US antitrust, it is not given an independent normative role. It is used instead to apply the exemptions of Article 101(3), so the analysis is significantly more structured than is often the case in the US. In it, the individual conditions of exemption are the focus, and the Commission uses presumptions to increase the structuring of the analysis.

Vertical agreements: The same basic criteria are used to assess vertical agreements that are used for cartel agreements, but applying the criteria is more complicated for three main reasons. First, as noted in Chapter 5, economic analysis itself is more complicated in the case of vertical agreements, because more than one market is involved, so the relationships that can cause harm are more difficult to discern. Second, economic analysis is applied within the structures of the treaty rather than as an independent legal standard. If an agreement does not fit within one of the exemptions, it violates the treaty. And third, European markets are often highly concentrated, which increases the likelihood that power in one market can be used to cause harm in another market. The concentration of markets also increases sensitivity to the use of power, particularly at the political level, so it also increases the impetus to pursue these targets.

Abuse of dominance: Some of these factors also influence the treatment of unilateral conduct (abuse of a dominant position).

The law is more structured than in some countries. Markets must be clearly defined; dominance must be established; and relatively specific criteria of abuse must be met. Yet the focus on power that has been central to the evolution of competition law in Europe throughout its development provides an openness to considering new forms of power. Most notable here is the willingness to consider the control of data and the size of the firms controlling large amounts of data (e.g., Google and Facebook) in assessing abuse of dominance. In addition, high levels of government involvement in the economy have combined with the relatively small size of most European national economies to create dominant firms in many markets. Some are supported by national governments as "national champions." The result is that the conduct of dominant firms is a major focus of competition law thought and enforcement.

Mergers: The merger control component of competition law was introduced long after the Rome treaty because it was long resisted by some member states. Resistance to the application of merger law has not disappeared but it has diminished significantly. The Commission assesses mergers under a Merger Regulation which is authorized by the treaty, but not included in it.[6] Economic harm is the primary consideration in this area as well, but openness to other elements of power mentioned above—for example, control over data—is also evident here. Horizontal mergers tend to receive the most attention, and here economics plays a role similar to its role in the US, so that concentration levels are a key part of the analysis, but a broader conception of power that includes power over data leads to greater attention to these issues not only in assessing horizontal mergers, but in the areas of vertical and conglomerate mergers as well.

F. GLOBAL ROLES

EU competition law plays global roles similar to those played by US antitrust. Each has political and economic leverage that

---

[6] Council Regulation (EC) No. 139/2004 on the control of concentrations between undertakings (EC Merger Regulation) [2004] OJ L24/1.

it uses to influence other competition law systems, and each enforces its law extraterritorially, assuring that lawyers, firms, and enforcers everywhere must pay attention to what it says and does. The EU's global role is shaped by three additional elements.

One is Europe's legal, cultural, and historical relationships with other legal systems. Most foreign competition law regimes in Latin America, Africa, and southern Asia are part of legal systems based on European (i.e., civil law) traditions and patterns. As a result, they often have institutions that are similar to European institutions, follow procedures that are similar to European procedures, and use concepts and assumptions that are drawn from European legal systems. This facilitates understanding, making messages easier to comprehend and reducing the likelihood of misunderstandings. In general, this tends to support European competition law's influence in these regimes.

Second, competition law in Europe has faced problems similar to those faced by many newer competition law regimes. During the twentieth century, many European countries moved from economically weak, centralized economies with large elements of state control to market economies, and to varying degree they used competition law as a tool to construct the competition culture that underpinned the market economy. Throughout this evolution European competition law has had to compete for legitimacy and support with entrenched attitudes favoring an active role for the state in the economy. In contrast to the US, it could not merely "enforce the law," but had to generate acceptance for it. In the twenty-first century many countries face the same challenges, so the European experience can be highly valuable for them.

And third, EU competition law directly influences several other competition law regimes. For example, Switzerland, Norway, and the UK are not part of the EU, but they have aligned their competition laws with it to minimize disruption in trade and investment between their competition law regimes and the EU's. Also, the EU must approve the competition law of any state that seeks admission to the EU, and a requirement of admission is that an applicant's competition law align with that of the EU. This

means that all states that have applied for membership or expect
to do so in the future must follow the EU model.

The importance and influence of EU competition law
has grown significantly, and the contrasts and perspectives it
contributes are likely to continue to grow in importance.

10

OTHER COMPETITION
LAWS: SHAPING FACTORS

More than a hundred other competition law regimes are part of
the global competition law system—some as major players, some
at the margins. Before the 1990s most did not even exist or played
only marginal roles in legal and business life. The extension and
deepening of globalization since then has dramatically changed
the landscape. One result is that most regimes are relatively
young. They are still fashioning goals, methods, and practices that
serve their own objectives.

This chapter does not present in-depth information about individual competition law regimes. There are far too many for
that. Moreover, these individual regimes do not play the kinds of
leading roles in the global system that US and European competition laws play. Instead, the chapter identifies factors that shape
all competition law regimes. These "shaping factors" serve as
guideposts that highlight relevant information about a regime
("here's where to look") and lead us to the most valuable and
useful questions to ask to understand it better. They cut through
the thicket of data to what we need to know. Noting these
factors and their influence can be of great value in looking at
any regime! The objective is not to provide details, but to pen-
etrate the details, make sense of them, and guide entry into and
through them.

Often specific factors shape an entire group (or family) of
regimes. These "shared shaping factors" help us recognize
similarities and differences among regimes within the group
and to see how they relate to each other. The Guide discusses
three examples: East Asia, Latin America, and emerging market
countries.

Competition Law and Antitrust. David J. Gerber, Oxford University Press (2020). © David J. Gerber.
DOI: 10.1093/oso/9780198727477.001.0001

A. SHAPING FACTORS

Legal, economic, political, and social factors inevitably shape competition laws. They provide the assumptions and incentives that frame and drive decisions, so they are often indispensable for understanding past decisions and predicting future ones.

1. THE DOMESTIC ECONOMY

Political leaders enact a competition law to benefit their own society (or, occasionally, themselves) so the characteristics of the domestic economy inevitably influence its contents. How big is the economy? How open is it to trade and investment? What does it produce and buy? Answers to such questions often illuminate competition law decisions.

Size: It influences the structure and intensity of competition. For example, a larger economy generally supports larger markets with more potential competitors, and it may create more opportunities for expansion and diversification. Opponents of competition law sometimes claim that it has little value in such an economy, particularly where the market is open, because market forces will eventually eliminate any restrictions on competition that might exist—an attitude not uncommon in the US, for example. Smaller markets, in contrast, are typically more susceptible to dominance and manipulation, which creates greater potential for abusive conduct.

Income levels: Where income levels are relatively high, more is available for consumers to spend and individuals and companies to invest. This influences the types and amounts of goods and services consumers purchase and tends to generate new enterprises and to sharpen competition. Lower income levels, on the other hand, are often associated with weaker competition in many sectors of the economy and more concern for protecting domestic producers.

Openness: An economy's openness to foreign trade and investment tends to increase the intensity of competition on its markets. This may reduce the perceived need for competition law to protect against restraints, but sometimes it also creates incentives to use competition law to control foreign influence in the economy. These incentives can be significant, particularly in a smaller, less economically developed country that wants to support its domestic producers.

Technological development: An economy with many successful technology companies is likely to have higher levels of investment and innovation, because these are normally necessary to achieve technological leadership. This is associated with more competitive markets and better competitive positions on international markets. The country's competition concerns often focus, therefore, on cartels among larger firms and their potential for consumer harm. In contrast, officials in a technologically less developed economy often have incentives to protect their own producers, so they may pay less attention to cartels, especially those among domestic enterprises, and pay greater attention to abuses of power, particularly by foreign firms.

Economic factors such as these influence not only goals and enforcement priorities, but also institutions and methods. A larger economy can provide more extensive resources for its enforcement agency than a small or weak economy, enabling it to acquire more effective enforcement tools as well as better trained and more experienced officials for using them.

2. SOCIETY

What is the social structure? What are the political and economic elites? How closed are they? Who talks with whom? Who has status? How are groups allied with each other? Answers to such questions can help us understand how a competition law regime actually functions. Where, for example, political power, social influence, and wealth in a society are firmly embedded in a small elite, that group's interests will influence the choice of targets and the intensity with which they are pursued. Decision-makers from that elite group may have few incentives to aggressively pursue firms controlled by other members of the group.

These incentives are sometimes offset by other considerations. For example, members of the elite may see their own positions threatened by social unrest and believe that it would be in their own interest to emphasize competition law's role in promoting fairness and protecting the competitive opportunities of small and medium-size domestic firms. Societal factors are seldom discussed in formal treatments of competition law, but there is often much value in identifying them.

3. CULTURE AND RELIGION

Cultural and religious values shape attitudes toward both competition and law, and knowing even a small amount about either of them can be illuminating. For example, religious institutions typically seek to foster "community" values and, therefore, see competition as a threat to their goals. This may inhibit support for competition law and/or generate support for goals such as fairness. Although such influences tend to be marginal in more industrialized societies, especially in the West, they are often a significant factor in emerging market economies.

General cultural values can play similar roles. For example, many in areas with a history of foreign or class domination distrust markets, because they fear that the markets are manipulated by those with economic or political power, particularly foreigners. As a result, they tend to see little value in government efforts to protect a process they distrust. In contrast, the high cultural value attached to the process of competition in the US is a key to understanding the political support antitrust has usually enjoyed there.

4. THE POLITICAL CONTEXT

The levels, forms, and directions of domestic support for competition law can be central to a government's choice of goals and enforcement priorities. Several questions can be particularly useful for assessing the political context. (1) How stable is the political situation? Volatile regimes tend to focus on short-term issues (like staying in power) and rarely give serious support to tools such as competition law whose benefits are likely to be realized (if ever) over a longer period. In some cases, however, a ruling group may use competition law to promote its short-term political objectives (e.g., to punish its rivals). (2) How corrupt are the bureaucracy and the courts, and is the corruption widely known in the society?

This is a major issue in many systems. A Competition Authority (CA) in which officials receive benefits from business firms is unlikely to take serious enforcement action against its benefactors. Similarly, more than a few CAs have been frustrated by corruption in reviewing courts. Where such corruption is well known or suspected in the society, public support for competition law suffers. (3) "Which political institutions can and do influence competition law?" In a democracy, the will of "the people"—typically, as expressed by a fairly elected legislature—is expected to be the primary influence. In an authoritarian regime, however, the rulers can control the law for their own purposes, making it an instrument of power. This tends to subvert the operation of competition law. Sometimes the extent of authoritarian influence is not easily seen, but it deserves careful attention.

5. THE DOMESTIC LEGAL SYSTEM

Each competition law regime functions according to the basic principles of the domestic legal system of which it is part, so recognizing these principles often tells us much about how competition law itself functions.

Perceiving law: Basic perceptions of law often profoundly influence competition law. In some societies, for example, law functions as a distinct and largely independent decision-making domain in which legal principles are applied by independent institutions following established legal methods. Here decisions of competition law institutions tend, therefore, to be relatively predictable. In many other countries, however, law is basically understood to be a tool by which government seeks its objectives rather than an independent principles-based domain. This makes decisions more difficult to assess and predict. Such background characteristics are critical to the way competition law functions, but they are often overlooked, because they are not specific to competition law.

Law's voices: Law can speak with many voices, so it is important to know which ones are likely to influence particular competition law institutions and their decisions. For example, in some legal systems, courts have particularly high status and significant discretion in interpreting, applying, and sometimes creating the law. Judicial "voices" are, therefore, particularly important for competition law. In others the legislature's voice has the most prominent status, and courts have limited space for interpretation. Sometimes, administrative institutions (e.g., in Japan) enjoy particularly high status, so here one can expect the CA to be the dominant "voice" in competition law.

6. GLOBAL ROLES AND RELATIONS

A competition law regime's relationships with other regimes often influence its decisions. We will look at these global relationships in more detail later, but a few factors deserve note here:

One is the degree to which a government and/or its CA depends on foreign sources for aid or other support. Where the government relies on foreign investment, for example, this inevitably affects the choices it makes for competition law. It may enact legislation designed to assure foreign investors that it will be "welcoming" to them. It may also direct enforcement efforts toward or away from certain targets that are likely to deter such investments. Similarly, the government may itself need economic support in the form of aid or political support, and this may give representatives of potential donor countries influence over decisions of the country's CA.

These relationships can also have less obvious results. For example, recipient regimes may pay homage to Western models in their official statements, but give more weight to domestic needs and interests when they make decisions. This tends to increase the gap between the law "on the books" and the law "in practice," obscuring what is actually influencing decisions in that regime. This can sometimes be seen by comparing a CA's English language website with the domestic language version of the website. In the English language website a CA or government may make one set of claims about the country's goals and practices, while it makes rather different claims on the domestic language website. An outsider should, therefore, be cautious about the value of public statements intended for foreign audiences and verify their value with those who know what is actually happening in the regime in question.

B. SHARED SHAPING FACTORS

Identifying shaping factors that are central to a group of regimes can be particularly useful. They point to what is significant and influential in the group, and they enable us to use what we know about one regime to know what to look for in others. Both similarities and differences deserve attention and drive us to questions about why they exist. Three examples demonstrate how we can use this idea to gain insights into individual regimes and relationships among regimes.

1. EAST ASIA: EMBEDDED, POLITICALLY SUPPORTED BUREAUCRACY

The bureaucracy plays a central role in the competition laws of East Asia (China, Japan, and Korea). Bureaucracies are important in most competition laws, but they are especially influential in this group, because the bureaucracies are both "*embedded*" and "*politically supported*." They are "politically supported" in the sense that they have the support of the political leadership, whatever its ideology and characteristics may be; they are "embedded," because they are deeply ingrained in society and culture, and their status has been reinforced over a significant period of time. Many bureaucracies feature one or the other of these characteristics, but outside East Asia few have both.

The set of ideas that supports and embeds the bureaucracy in East Asia is often referred to as "Confucian," although we must use the term cautiously. It includes the following ideas: (1) Society is organic—that is, each part or group within it is inherently related to all others; (2) the bureaucracy plays a leading role in society, and bureaucrats have correspondingly high social status; (3) societal harmony is highly valued in relation to individual freedom; (4) harmony is maintained through structured mutual obligations and duties; and (5) education enjoys high status and reinforces hierarchical structures.

These ideas have animated East Asian cultures for some two millennia. They took shape in China, and their influence has remained powerful throughout the region—sometimes until well into the nineteenth century. Although that influence has waned since then, it remains considerable in some areas of political and legal life even in the twenty-first century. Countries within the group differ in important ways, but what we can call "East Asian bureaucratic centralism" remains a core element of each.

a. China

Contexts: After more than a century of disruption caused by military weakness, technological stagnation, and violent political upheavals, the Chinese bureaucracy re-emerged after 1949—now as the core institution of Chinese communism. It maintains features from the earlier bureaucratic tradition, but it has added a parallel bureaucracy—the Party (i.e., the Chinese Communist Party). The two bureaucracies are intertwined, and Party officials frequently play roles that parallel those of their government counterparts. Higher bureaucrats and judges must also be members of the Party.

This intertwined bureaucracy is interwoven with large segments of the economy in complex ways. Ministries in Beijing as well as local and provincial bureaucracies often participate in major enterprises, creating incentives to protect the market positions and well-being of those enterprises. As a result, managers and officials sometimes see competition law as a potential threat to their capacity to control markets. The influence of these ties to the economy on competition law decisions is difficult to see, and there are few incentives for bureaucrats to reveal them.

This framework of values nevertheless creates risks for the bureaucracy. The cultural tradition calls for "reciprocal" obligations: the people owe obedience, but the rulers (i.e., the Party) owe them protection in exchange. Lurking in the background for Chinese decision-makers is awareness that the population expects the bureaucracy to provide economic growth and high employment and that ultimately its fate rests on support from the population. This context shapes competition law, and outsiders often fail to recognize its influence.

The Antimonopoly Law (AML): China enacted its first competition law in 2007 after a decade of discussions within the bureaucracy.[1] It was based primarily on European models, but interpretation and enforcement have also been influenced by US antitrust law.

Goals: The AML's formal goals represent messages from the bureaucracy to both external and internal audiences. They tell foreign governments and international institutions that China seeks basically the same goals that they seek, but they reassure internal audiences that the Party and bureaucracy are seeking to improve the people's welfare by creating economic growth and advancing the "socialist market economy." The CA takes both goals seriously in implementing the AML, but the Party can change direction at will, so it is important to pay attention to recent changes in its formulation of goals.

Institutions and methods: The CA is part of the bureaucracy, which means that the Party can control it. This does not mean, however, that the Party *does* control all decisions. Many decisions have little or no political relevance, and the Party therefore pays correspondingly little attention to them. Moreover, the bureaucracy knows that allowing competition law to operate primarily "as law" (in the Western sense) can bring benefits for China. It tends to legitimize Chinese law in the eyes of others, and this helps to generate higher status for the competition law and greater confidence among foreign investors.

The CA uses methods drawn primarily from the US and Europe. Its methods of interpreting texts are based largely on European models, although they are not always applied as rigorously as in countries such as Germany, and the goals of the "socialist market economy" can provide an ideological element absent in the West. In addition, officials are often highly competent in economic analysis. In general, however, the CA reveals little about its reasoning, so it is important for system-outsiders to seek advice from those with "insider insights." Courts can review the CA's decisions, but they are also subject to Party control so they are unlikely to create significant conflicts with the CA.

---

[1] Zhonghua Renmin Gongheguo Fan Longduan Fa [Anti-Monopoly Law of the People's Republic of China] (promulgated by the Standing Comm. Nat'l People's Cong., August 30, 2007, effective August 1, 2008) CLI.1.96789(EN) (Lawinfochina).

Substantive law and targets: The substantive law is based on European, particularly German, sources, but here again the CA's embeddedness in the central bureaucracy and its social market economy principles leads to variations in application. It also means that changes in general economic policy can lead to changes in interpreting the law and in enforcement targets, and there is often little external notice of the changes. Examining the CA's current practices in the context of general government policy can be valuable. In particular, the bureaucracy typically pays much attention to protecting and supporting Chinese firms, so foreign acquisition of Chinese firms is often scrutinized. Similarly, the bureaucracy's ties to dominant firms tend to limit enforcement against Chinese dominant firms and increase incentives to enforce against their foreign competitors. In some areas, Chinese Supreme Court interpretations are also influential, notably in the highly circumscribed sphere of private enforcement.

Global roles: China's political and economic weight gives the bureaucracy potentially significant influence on foreign competition laws, particularly in Asia and emerging markets.

b. Japan and South Korea

Japan and South Korea locate bureaucratic centralism in more open and democratically contested political systems. The competition law regimes differ from each other in many important respects, but we treat them together here in order to sharpen our insights into the similarities and differences.

Contexts: Both Japan and Korea are high income, highly industrialized, and technologically advanced countries. The economies depend heavily on exports and overseas investment by their companies. Domestically, "wheel and spokes" structures (*keiretsu* in Japan; *chaebol* in Korea) play significant, though diminishing roles. In this structure a bank and one or more major industrial firms are typically at the center of a network of smaller firms that provide supplies and support to the industrial firm in return for support obligations from the center. This provides economic stability and supports the growth of high-tech exports, but it also gives the central firms extensive influence over the dependent ones. These relationships reflect long-established patterns of hierarchy and mutual obligation.

Both political systems are democratic and feature powerful central bureaucracies and independent courts. In contrast to China, however, the bureaucracy's power here is not monolithic. It is constrained by other institutions and by a political system that requires the bureaucracy to explain and justify its decisions.

Competition law: The respective competition laws are active and internationally respected. Each is deeply embedded in a powerful and firmly established bureaucracy. As a result, they are influenced by the general economic policies of the bureaucracy, but they operate primarily according to legal principles and procedures. The political contexts create pressures on the CAs that differ from those in China.

For Japan, a bit of history highlights the bureaucracy's role. US occupying forces imposed competition law there after the Second World War, but for many decades the bureaucracy did very little to enforce it. It was following an economic strategy that was antithetical to competition law goals, focusing instead on a central role for the bureaucracy (MITI) in guiding economic development. The CA (Japan Fair Trade Commission, JFTC) was given little support—either financial or political. But the globalization of the 1990s led to a fundamental change. The government now enlisted competition law *in the service of* economic development and made it an important feature of its economic policy.[2] The government significantly increased support for the CA, and this led to more enforcement, higher fines, and a more central role in the economy. In effect, the bureaucracy's central role and embeddedness allowed it to change competition law significantly as its understanding of Japanese interests changed.

Korean competition law experience shows similarities, but also differences. Since the end of military rule in the 1980s, the political system has become strongly democratic, as social-democratically inspired governments have alternated with conservative, non-interventionist ones. The role and power of the chaebols has often been a central issue in the political arena, and much of the debate

---

[2] Ministry of Foreign Affairs of Japan, 'The Deregulation Action Program' (*Ministry of Foreign Affairs of Japan*, March 31, 1995) <https://www.mofa.go.jp/policy/economy/summit/1996/recent/program.html> accessed November 4, 2019.

has focused on competition law's role in controlling chaebol power. Fluctuation in political leadership between those who are avowedly business friendly and those who are more willing to control business often creates treacherous waters for the Korean CA (Korea Fair Trade Commission). As in Japan, there is respect for legal institutions and methods ("the rule of law"). In Korea the CA must deal with courts that are quite willing to reverse its decisions. In particular, it must operate within a tension between the powerful chaebols and popular resentment to their power. In addition, it must respond to perceived unfairness in their control of dependent smaller firms, but it is under political pressure not to take action that would impede the chaebols' capacity to compete internationally. Since the 1990s the legislature has significantly strengthened competition law and the legal institutions implementing it.

The competition law statutes in the two regimes also differ significantly. The Japanese Antimonopoly Law (AML) is modeled on US antitrust principles dictated by postwar Occupation authorities, but the legal system is based primarily on European principles.[3] This has led to much complexity in interpreting and applying the statute. It has also underscored the role of the bureaucracy as a source of consistency and a repository of knowledge as well as the importance of scholars in deciphering its complexity.

The Korean statute is more recent and more firmly based on European (basically German) models.[4] It was produced through a democratic process and adapted to the Korean context. The bureaucracy's institutions have been central in interpreting and applying the statute, but courts and commentators also play major roles in interpreting it. Private enforcement is available in both systems, but incentives to sue are comparatively limited, particularly in Japan, where procedural obstacles and cultural factors tend to inhibit private litigation.

Both domestic and global economic considerations influence enforcement targets. Reliance on exports by large producers tends

---

[3] Act on Prohibition of Private Monopolization and Maintenance of Fair Trade (Act No. 54 of April 14, 1947).

[4] Monopoly Regulation and Fair Trade Act, Law No. 3320, December 31, 1980.

to discourage both CAs from taking significant enforcement action against dominant domestic firms where such actions might harm their capacity to compete internationally. This reliance also tends to give a more central role to the bureaucracy in competition contexts on the assumption that it is in the best position to evaluate the consequences of competition law decisions in the international arena and to negotiate with foreign governments and firms regarding Japanese interests.

The shaping power of the central bureaucracy is evident in each of these regimes, and comparing them reveals how differing political, social, and economic contexts mold its roles.

2. SOCIALLY CONCENTRATED POWER: LATIN AMERICA

The concentration of economic and political power in a small social group represents a second central shaping factor. It has been a prominent feature in Latin American societies, and recognizing its influence highlights patterns in the region.

Socially concentrated power: The concentration of wealth, political power, social status, and economic control in Latin America has deep roots. The Spanish and Portuguese who conquered the continent in the sixteenth century divided the land among themselves, granting very large tracts to a few individuals who used it in large-scale agriculture and the extraction of raw materials. These small elites controlled political power and dominated both society and education. When colonialism ended in the early nineteenth century, this basic pattern often continued. Only gradually have others acquired property and influence. The middle class has typically remained relatively small in many countries, primarily because economic activity has centered on agriculture and extractive industries rather than on commerce and entrepreneurship. This centralization of wealth and power often generates resentment among other members of society, and at times it fosters conflict.

This social and economic structure has generally marginalized the role of competition, although that is rapidly changing in some countries. It was further submerged in the process of industrialization by ideologies based on government control of the economy.

During the second half of the twentieth century, major Latin American governments pursued a policy of *dependencia*. The central idea was that government had to protect domestic producers from bigger and more advanced competitors from the US and Europe, so they should replace imports with domestic production. This policy benefitted those in control, and it did preserve a measure of economic independence—for a time, but it eventually also led to very high inflation rates and increasing economic stagnation, which fueled periodic military dictatorships and political instability.

Competition law: These factors obscured the value of competition law until the 1990s. Since then, however, economic globalization and the rise of more democratic political regimes has kindled a significant increase in interest in many countries. Members of the elite increasingly came to see competition law as a tool they could use to their own benefit and the benefit of their societies. It could help integrate their domestic economies into the global economy. This view links competition law to the capacity of domestic firms to compete in global markets, and it can give their governments a greater role in global economic relations.

Generalizing about Latin America's competition law regimes is hazardous, because they differ from each other significantly and can change frequently. Two patterns are, however, worth noting. First, tensions and interplays among traditional elites, increasingly significant middle classes, and weaker groups who seek greater economic benefits and economic and political participation are central to the evolution of most regimes. Second, complex relations with the US and Europe sometimes play pivotal roles in this story. The legal regimes are based on European models and practices, and social and economic ties to Europe have often been strong, but the influence of US antitrust law has grown since the 1990s, especially in a few leading countries. However, this influence is itself sometimes colored by the history of US involvement in Latin America, which has at times involved direct political and even military intervention to deter Latin American countries from veering too far from US political and economic agendas. This has often led to significant resentment and resistance in segments of Latin American populations.

Goals: Countries that seek to play more important roles in the global economy and the competition law system—for example, Chile, Colombia, Brazil, Peru, and Argentina—have incentives to follow OECD models that focus on economic goals, primarily consumer welfare, and efficiency goals. This sends a message to foreign governments and institutions about their investment-friendly intentions and aspirations. Often, however, domestic groups demand greater attention to fairness and other political and social goals, and some regimes make efforts to respond to these demands.

Methods and institutions: Regimes that focus on economic goals necessarily use economic methods of analysis, but CAs in many countries are new and underfunded, making it difficult to attract and maintain high-level staff and preventing the full use of advanced economic methods. As a result, many cannot pursue economic analysis as rigorously as it is pursued in the US and Europe. Moreover, many judges tend to resist emphasis on economic analysis and rely instead on traditional legal analysis.

Several factors tend to limit support for competition law institutions. First, corruption is common and assumed in some countries, inhibiting reliance on government institutions. Second, many are skeptical of competition itself, in part because relatively few participate in competitive markets or see how they might benefit from competition. And third, many groups assume that the elite—either alone or in conjunction with foreign interests—control markets.

Substantive law and enforcement: Statutes are generally based on European models, but US influence can sometimes be seen in interpretation and enforcement. Where economic goals are prominent, the focus is usually on horizontal agreements—particularly transnational cartels. Many regimes pay attention to abuse of dominance, primarily because it is seen as a means of combating inflation, which is often a major concern in the region. In general, competition law tends to be lightly enforced, but enforcement can increase rapidly where both elite and middle-class interests support it.

Global roles: Most Latin American countries still play relatively marginal roles in the global competition law system. Few others look to them for guidance, and as individual regimes they have limited political and economic leverage. A few competition law regimes—for example, Brazil and Chile, have however become respected players in the global competition law system.

Socially concentrated power has shaped the evolution of competition law in these countries, and it provides valuable insights into their dynamics.

3. Emerging Markets: The Development Imperative

Economic development is central to competition law in emerging market countries (EMCs). Each regime confronts two major challenges. One is to decide how competition law can serve that goal. The other is the need to balance the desire for long-term economic development against the short-term benefits of meeting the demands of foreign firms and institutions. Development is a long-term project in which domestic producers inevitably play an important role, but protecting producers clashes with the consumer welfare-based competition law models favored by capital-exporting countries.

Colonial control and impeded development: Most emerging market countries were European colonies, and colonial relationships tended to impede development. In many, colonial rule lasted into the 1960s and even later, particularly in Africa. It left a legacy of stunted development, because colonial powers had extracted resources for themselves, but often paid little attention to the local population. They did little to provide education, and they often eliminated indigenous legal traditions and institutions. In Africa, even the states and their borders were created by Europeans.

The legacy has left many societies with low income levels, inefficient infrastructures, and limited capacity to compete outside their own territory. Many have continued to rely on the export of primary agricultural products and minerals, because they have not been in a position to develop large-scale or tech-based industries. Colonialism's legacy has also undermined the development of strong and stable political institutions. "Rule of law" deficiencies are common.

Hesitant support for competition law: These and other factors have impeded competition law development. Many in these populations have had limited experience of competition other than in local markets, and perceptions of foreign and class control of markets lead some to be skeptical of its value and to prefer government intervention such as price controls. Seeing little value in competition, they see little point in protecting it, particularly if foreign interests can be expected manipulate it.

Other factors tend to enhance skepticism about competition law. Many competition laws have been enacted under foreign pressure or even drafted by former colonial rulers. Some were enacted soon after independence on the model of the former colonial power, and there is little evidence that there was a serious intent to implement them. Other statutes were enacted as a condition for receiving loans from the World Bank or other international lending agency. These factors suggest to many that the laws are not intended to serve the needs of the domestic population. As a result, there is often little popular understanding and support for competition law, implementation is often limited, and statutes may be applied in ways that have little to do with the statute's text.

Goals: Formal goal statements need to be viewed with caution. They are not always reliable guides to decisions. In addition to the factors mentioned above that can inhibit serious implementation, countries often have strong incentives to use competition law statutes as messages to foreign governments and investors that the country is committed to a market economy and "rule of law." This can lead them to adopt "Western" goal statements without a serious intention to pursue them. Particularly where government leaders are allied or identical with domestic producers, the institutions tend to pay greater attention to their interests than is common in other regimes. Some statutes (e.g., South Africa) do emphasize fairness goals and acknowledge the goal of protecting small and medium-sized businesses.[5]

Institutions and methods: CAs typically have limited resources and low levels of political, social, and intellectual support. They often employ methods similar to those used in Western regimes,

---

[5] Competition Act [No. 89 of 1998], at 2.(*e*).

but their limited resources mean that the methods may be used in unpredictable ways. Officials are often underpaid and thus potentially susceptible to corruption, and their training is often limited. This not only contributes to the sometimes questionable use of methods, but it also means a government may not be in a position to enforce its competition law against powerful economic interests, especially where it needs foreign investment.

Targets: Development needs are often reflected in decisions about competition law targets.

Horizontal agreements: These are common targets, but there are often significant exceptions for cooperation among domestic firms, especially smaller ones. They are seen as potential engines of economic development, so cartels of small and medium-sized firms are sometimes given special status either formally or in practice.

Vertical agreements: In EMCs, they often involve foreign firms that use local firms to distribute their products. In these cases CAs must weigh the benefits to domestic distributors and consumers of having access to the foreign goods against potential harm from provisions in the agreements that limit development benefits—for example, by requiring a distributor to follow directions from the manufacturer regarding prices, territories, and customers or to grant the manufacturer rights to any improvements the domestic distributor may make in the products. Where a regime gives priority to development goals it is likely to target and pursue these agreements.

Unilateral conduct: There is often concern about the effects of foreign dominant firms, but there has been relatively limited enforcement against them, except where a dominant foreign firm clearly appears to be hindering domestic economic development. Enforcement can be tempered by the need for foreign investment. Typically, a domestic CA will be very cautious about taking significant enforcement steps against such firms. It is more likely to negotiate with them about mitigating development harms.

Mergers: Development needs, minimal economic leverage, lack of resources for analyzing effects, and the perceived need for foreign investment generally inhibit CAs from blocking mergers. Mergers among domestic firms are often seen as valuable for economic development, and blocking an acquisition by a foreign firm eliminates the domestic development benefits that such a merger may bring. Where the domestic market is sufficiently attractive to foreign investors, however, the CA will have some weight in negotiations with potential foreign acquirers.

Competition law's evolution: Despite these obstacles, the twenty-first century has seen noteworthy competition law activity in some countries (e.g., South Africa and Kenya), particularly where leaders have come to see competition law as a tool of economic development that can benefit them as well as support the economic and social progress of their societies. Interest has increased in many other countries, and the educational infrastructure to support further progress is being put in place.

Global roles: Emerging market regimes seldom have sufficient economic and political leverage by themselves to play major roles in the global system. Their markets are often small, at least in terms of purchasing power, giving them little opportunity to apply their laws extraterritorially. Moreover, their lack of experience with competition law and the still relatively low levels of support for it generally mean that they rely on foreign CAs and international organizations for both advice and support. Regional cooperation is increasingly seen as a potential basis for increasing this role, as the growing importance of COMESA (Common Market for East and South Africa) shows.[6]

This part has looked at individual competition law regimes, highlighting the factors that drive decisions in them and some of the ways they interact with each other. It has also identified the kinds of questions that need to be asked in seeking to better understand them. Finally, it has provided tools for seeing similarities and differences among competition law firms and identifying shared shaping factors. The final part builds on this information and on these insights as we look at how competition law regimes are related together across the globe.

---

[6] COMESA, 'COMESA Objectives and Priorities' (*COMESA*) < https://www.comesa.int/company-overview-2/> accessed November 4, 2019.

PART IV

GLOBAL DYNAMICS AND FORCES OF CHANGE

This final part focuses on competition law's global dimensions and on forces that challenge both individual regimes and the global system. Chapter 11 shows how domestic regimes, transnational institutions, and private interest groups interact to shape competition law. They form part of a global system with its own patterns and dynamics, and recognizing how this system works helps to understand, interpret, and predict those decisions. Chapter 12 unravels the ways that globalization and the digital economy challenge competition law and highlights responses to those challenges.

11

THE GLOBAL SYSTEM: INTERACTING AND ADAPTING

The previous chapters have identified many individual instances in which cross-border influences and interactions affect competition law decisions. We have seen how arguments, methods, claims, and decisions in one regime often influence what others in other regimes think, say, and do. If we want to make sense of this maze of interactions, we have to see how the pieces fit together and relate to each other. This chapter provides a kind of map of the territory that shows us the pathways through the maze. It presents the individual interactions and influences as parts of a whole. This makes competition law decisions everywhere more comprehensible and more predictable, so it can be extraordinarily useful.

The key to doing this is recognizing that the web of interactions constitutes an "adaptive system." We will see what that means. The term "global system" is typically used in loose and vague ways to refer to what's happening "outside our borders." Until recently, that may have been appropriate, but it now misses or obscures much of what we need to know—that is, how the pieces fit together! In this chapter we use "system" in a more specific way! Deep globalization and the digital restructuring of communication and transportation have generated an interactive and adaptive system that has patterns, rules, and structures of its own. Being aware of this system and how it functions enables us to see what we did not see before! It gives us more insight into what has happened in the past and a better basis for predicting what is likely to happen in the future.

We first outline the formal framework of the system—the basic rules that guide and constrain states in applying their laws to conduct outside their borders. We then look at the system in motion—how ideas, incentives, and pressures cross regime borders to shape and drive decisions.

Competition Law and Antitrust. David J. Gerber, Oxford University Press (2020). © David J. Gerber.
DOI: 10.1093/oso/9780198727477.001.0001

A. JURISDICTION: THE FRAMEWORK OF THE SYSTEM

The concept of jurisdiction is central to the formal framework within which competition laws relate to each other. "Jurisdiction" refers to *legitimate authority*. It is a "yes or no" principle: you either have it or you don't. Our concern here is with the authority of a state to regulate private conduct. The principles used to define this authority have been developed over centuries by the states themselves in order to distribute authority and reduce conflicts. They are often referred to as part of "customary international law." States almost always follow them, principally because without them a state could do whatever it wanted to do unless challenged by force or pressure not to do it. The more powerful players would control conduct—not law. Few wish that outcome. Some prefer not to think of these principles as "law" because they are not "enforceable" by armies or police forces. What is important in practice is that states generally follow them.

1. JURISDICTIONAL PRINCIPLES

The basic idea behind jurisdiction in this context is that a state is authorized to apply its laws to those with whom it has a sufficiently close connection (i.e., its jurisdictional "base"). One connection is territory—a state has authority to control conduct on its own territory. Territory cannot be replicated, so this principle is unlikely to lead to overlapping claims or create uncertainty and conflict. A second connection is nationality: a state is authorized to apply its laws to its own nationals (including corporations). These two principles can create jurisdictional conflicts (e.g., state A claims jurisdiction on the basis of territory and state B claims jurisdiction based on a firm's nationality) but such overlaps are rare. These were basically the only two principles followed until after the Second World War.

In the decades after the war, however, a third principle was gradually accepted in order to accommodate increasing transnational commerce, and it dramatically changed this picture. This so-called "effects" principle provides that a state may apply its law to conduct *outside its territory if the conduct has significant and at least foreseeable effects within its territory*. This greatly increases the likelihood of overlapping ("concurrent") jurisdiction that can cause uncertainty, cost, and conflict. A global cartel (e.g., the oil cartel—OPEC) can, for example, cause harm in many states, and the effects principle may give each the authority to apply its competition law to the conduct!

These principles apply to two distinct forms of state action, but they are often confused. We are interested in only one of them, but we need to note the other. Our concern here is with the authority of a state to *apply* its law to a private actor—that is, to validly claim that a person has violated its law and is subject to a penalty for doing so. This is prescriptive (or legislative) jurisdiction, and it plays a central role in competition law. The other type of jurisdiction refers to a state's authority to "enforce" its claims. States very rarely take actions (e.g., use of police or armies) to enforce their competition laws outside their own territory, so it is not our concern here.

It is also important not to confuse two very different uses of "international jurisdiction." We will use it to refer to a state's authority *under international law* to take certain types of action, but the term can also be used to refer to the authority a state grants to its own institutions to apply its own laws to foreign conduct. That use of the term refers to *domestic law*. For example, when a US statute specifies that US antitrust law applies to conduct that has a "direct, substantial and reasonably foreseeable" effect within the US, it is giving directions to US institutions. The term "international jurisdiction" is used in both contexts, but they differ from each other fundamentally. One is domestic law; the other is public international law.

2. SOME CONSEQUENCES OF THE JURISDICTIONAL FRAMEWORK

This framework has important consequences that are often misunderstood or overlooked.

Formal equality, but disparate impact: Formally, the framework is fair—all states have the same jurisdictional authority. In practice, however, a state's *capacity to use* its authority depends largely on its economic and political leverage—primarily, the size and importance of its market. For example, if the EU applies its competition law to conduct outside EU territory and assesses a fine against a foreign violator, the violator usually complies, because access to the EU market is valuable, and failure to comply would prevent or limit such access. In contrast, a small African country may wish to apply its law to the same type of conduct, but its market is likely to be too small to give it the necessary economic leverage: it would cost a violator little, if anything, to avoid the country.

Uncertainty: The effects principle can also create uncertainty. It may authorize numerous states to apply their laws to the same conduct—for example, a patent licensing arrangement involving emerging markets. The laws and enforcement practices of the states regarding the arrangement are likely to vary, so a firm must make decisions in the face of significant uncertainty about what it can do and what the risks are. It could pay for business and legal advice to reduce the uncertainty, but that could be very costly. Alternatively, it could engage in the conduct and hope that no state's laws will be applied or that compliance costs will be low. The uncertainty can have important consequences. For example, it sometimes leads firms not to license technology that could have benefitted not only the firm but consumers and others as well.

Costs: This uncertainty imposes both direct and indirect costs on firms. The direct costs are those a firm pays for advice about the risks. Indirect costs arise where a firm changes its plans in order to avoid the risks and thereby foregoes the potential benefits of conduct that makes economic sense.

Conflicts: Overlapping jurisdictional claims can also lead to conflicts. Where more than one state claims authority to control the same conduct, the two claims may clash. For example, state A may apply its competition law to prohibit cartel conduct on state B's territory because it raises prices on A's domestic market, but B may encourage the same conduct as a means of coordinating economic activity in support of economic development. These conflicts are often resolved through negotiations, but sometimes they disrupt commercial or even diplomatic relationships among the parties, so they can be very harmful. As transnational markets grow and the number of active competition regimes increases, the potential for such conflicts also grows.

B. THE SYSTEM IN MOTION: ADAPTING AND INTERACTING

Pressures, ideas, and influences flow through and around this formal framework, influencing decisions throughout the system. They are the system in motion. Increased communication and interaction among officials, legislators, and scholars from many regimes provide ever-widening channels for these flows.

It is an adaptive system, and recognizing this enables us to see the channels themselves and the ways in which they flow together to influence decisions. This is what enables us to see what we otherwise cannot see. This perspective has rewarded those who look at the natural and social worlds. The Guide adapts and uses it here to gain similar benefits for understanding competition law regimes and the decisions made in them.

An adaptive system has three basic elements: A field or arena in which interactions take place; the players (or "agents") who interact in this field; and the interactions among them. When we look at each element carefully, we begin to make sense out of what appears to be a mass of jumbled data about seemingly unrelated events and institutions.

1. THE FIELD OF INTERACTION

We focus here on competition law, so the field of interaction includes the decisions taken to combat restraints on competition. This includes decisions taken by competition law officials, states, courts, and other institutions for that purpose as well as actions by others (e.g., lobbyists, companies, lawyers, and economists) that seek to influence these state-based decisions. Specifying the field of interaction forces us to identify clearly what we actually want to know and to avoid the clutter of data that may not be relevant.

2. PLAYERS

The players include states that take these decisions and also transnational institutions, private organizations, and individuals that seek to influence them. Each pursues its own goals—sometimes cooperating with other players, sometimes competing. The players act independently, but their decisions are interconnected by their ties to a globalizing economy and a communications network that is itself a key element in transnational competition and a channel through which influences flow. The actions of each depend to some extent on their knowledge of what others do or can be expected to do.

a. States

The primary players are individual competition law regimes, because they wield state power to directly affect the conduct of firms.

Goals: States pursue both domestic and transnational goals. Chapter 3 reviewed domestic goals; here we look at goals from a transnational perspective. They vary widely, depending primarily on the state's economic and political positions and priorities. A few examples: (1) Some states pursue stability in transnational markets and in the political conditions surrounding them. This benefits transnational firms, which typically seek predictability in order to plan more effectively. (2) Other governments seek to protect their domestic firms from foreign competition that may stifle their development. (3) A third goal is to secure resources—often raw materials—for domestic firms. (4) Sometimes a state focuses on acquiring allies and establishing cooperative arrangements that it can use to achieve its economic and political goals. Often states combine these goals. Recognizing a state's transborder goals helps us to interpret and predict what it will do in making decisions about competition law.

Capacities: Some states are in a better position than others to effectively pursue their goals. A state may use economic leverage. For example, if country A's markets are attractive to firms in country B, A's government can use access to its markets as a means of inducing country B to accept its decisions, accede to its requests, or follow its lead. A state may also use whatever political (or even military) power it might have to achieve these goals. It may be in a position to use these tools on a global scale, but often it uses them primarily in a particular region (e.g., southern Africa) or within specific contexts of economic or political dependence such as postcolonial economic ties between states (e.g., the influence of France in some of its colonies in West Africa).

Formal actions: A state can pursue its goals through both formal and informal actions. Both can influence other states and competition law regimes and elicit responses from them.

Enforcing domestic law: Competition law enforcement plays an important role in these interactions. Jurisdictional principles authorize all states to apply their laws to conduct outside their borders under certain circumstances, but each must decide if and to what extent it uses that authority. If it does apply its competition law outside its own territory, it necessarily impacts the interests of one or more other states who must then decide whether and how to respond, often setting off a chain of further reactions. Following this chain can itself be highly valuable.

Conflict avoidance measures: States use several types of strategies to reduce the likelihood and extent of conflict with other states.

One is private international law ("conflicts of law" in the US). Most legal systems authorize some domestic institutions (usually courts) to apply foreign law rather than domestic law under specified circumstances. The underlying idea is that where a court in country A must resolve a dispute involving conduct or interests in country B, applying B's law rather than its own to the conduct may serve the interests of both litigants and the states involved. It may be more efficient and accurate for the litigants, and it may avoid conflicts among states. Sometimes these private international law principles are contained in elaborate and detailed statutes (common in Europe); sometimes they are relatively vague, flexible, and case-based (US).

Self-restraint measures: Some states, including the US, authorize courts not to apply domestic law extraterritorially under specified circumstances—for example, where the application may harm a foreign state's interests. Often referred to in the US as the doctrine of comity, it can give much discretion to domestic institutions, and it is not widely used.

Defensive measures: States occasionally enact laws in order to deter the exercise of jurisdiction by another state. For example, the UK enacted a statute that authorized a UK firm to go to court in the UK to "claw back" penalties imposed in a foreign court as a result of applying the foreign state's competition law to conduct in the UK by UK nationals.[1] Such laws are few and seldom applied.

Coordination: Formal actions may be cooperative rather than unilateral. States often make agreements with other states regarding competition law, and they often participate in transnational organizations that deal with competition law issues. Some agreements create a separate set of legal principles to be applied to economic relations between the parties. They often specify which country's competition law will be applied in specified situations. Some even specify the competition law rules to be applied in these relationships. This makes it extremely important to check for the existence of such agreements. They change the general rules, but they are easily overlooked!

Regional agreements regulate trade between states in a particular geographical area, and they often include competition law provisions in order to prevent states from circumventing the trade provisions. The EU evolved from such an agreement, and they have become more numerous in other regions. In Africa, COMESA—Common Market for East and South Africa—has plans to develop competition law throughout these regions, and some impressive first steps have been taken.[2] ASEAN (Association of South East Asian Nations) has similar plans.[3] In Latin America there have been several attempts to develop such arrangements among specific states, and some continue to move in that direction. In North America, the NAFTA agreement is well known.[4]

[1] Protection of Trading Interests Act 1980, s. 6., c. 11.

[2] COMESA, 'Treaty Establishing the Common Market for Eastern and Southern Africa' (*COMESA*, December 8, 1994) <https://www.comesa.int/wpcontent/uploads/2019/02/comesa-treaty-revised-20092012_with-zaire_final.pdf> accessed November 4, 2019.

[3] ASEAN, 'The ASEAN Declaration (Bangkok Declaration)' (*AESEAN*, August 8, 1967) <https://asean.org/the-asean-declaration-bangkok-declaration-bangkok-8-august-1967/> accessed November 4, 2019.

[4] North American Free Trade Agreement, US–Can.–Mex., December 8, 1993, 32 ILM 289 (1993).

Some of these regional agreements have elaborate competition law provisions and even create institutions to apply them to trade among the member states (e.g., COMESA).

Bilateral agreements (two parties) often focus on particular issues of trade between the parties—for example, specific products and problems, sometimes including social problems in one or both states (e.g., the drug trade in the US–Colombia agreement).[5] They are typically between a richer, more economically advanced country and an emerging market country. Some basically allow the stronger party to use its economic weight to secure benefits from the weaker party, including, for example, beneficial treatment of its firms under the latter's competition law. In these arrangements, the goal of the weaker party is often to gain access to a larger and richer market.

Some bilateral agreements produce cooperation in enforcing competition laws. Fostered by more rapid communications, these arrangements take several forms. They are usually embodied in simple documents (e.g., a memorandum of understanding—MOU) that provide a framework of cooperation. Some are general and create an obligation on each Competition Authority (CA) to cooperate with the other in enforcement efforts. Others specifically require that the CAs provide information to each other that might lead to detection of harmful conduct—for example, suspicious price movements. These are often quite limited in scope—for example, they do not require a CA to violate its domestic law or the rights of those involved. Some include the more far-reaching obligation that each state pursue competition harm that is actually caused in or to the other state (positive comity). These are not common, and they are seldom used even where they exist. Enforcement assistance agreements are not highly publicized, but they should be studied carefully, because they can have important practical effects.

---

[5] Office of the United States Trade Representation, 'United States–Columbia Free Trade Agreement' (*Office of the United States Trade Representation*, November 22, 2006) <https://ustr.gov/trade-agreements/free-trade-agreements/colombia-fta/final-text> accessed November 4, 2019.

The informal sphere: Competition law regimes also interact at the informal level—for example, through personal encounters, e-mails, and messages on social media.

Technological developments in both transportation and communication have greatly increased the speed, frequency, and influence of these informal interactions. Reducing the time frame in which individual participants respond to the actions and messages of others has made the system adaptive and interactive. The contexts of speed, reactivity, and shareability shape the way the players connect with and respond to each other. Recognizing this enables us to see how the system functions.

Knowing the other players: Central to these interactions is the question "What are the other players doing now or likely to do soon?" All are playing in the same arena—that is, developing and applying competition law, and each can significantly affect and be affected by what the others do and say. As a result, each wants to know what others are doing or are likely to do soon. Some exert pressure. Others seek to persuade or cajole. The effectiveness of these measures often calls for knowing as much as possible about the factors that influence these decisions. This knowledge is particularly valuable for those who are most affected by the decisions and actions of others. This type of knowing requires careful attention to social and political factors—not merely formal legal analysis. In this context, tools of comparison developed in comparative law and elsewhere can also be very valuable.

Pressure: States and CAs that possess some form of power or leverage can use it to exert pressure on others. For example, state A can exert pressure on state B to adopt particular goals or methods or to take specific actions. If it has sufficient economic leverage—perhaps an attractive market—over B, B will be induced to pay attention to these requests. The pressure may be aggressive ("Don't mess with my brother's or political sponsor's company") or more gentle ("If you make this change, we'll find a way to reward you"). The pressure may also be more subtle— "Please consider the potential value of the merger for your economy."

Persuasion: Persuasion is necessary where the target government is sufficiently powerful that pressure may be ineffective or even counterproductive (e.g., efforts to influence China). Efforts to persuade may be direct and specific: an argument to a foreign government or CA that a particular policy or measure is "better" generally or that it will serve that government's interests. They may also be less direct and more general: a well-funded CA may, for example, invite officials from a foreign CA to visit it or send junior employees for training.

b. Transnational organizations

Transnational organizations are important elements of the system. They do not directly influence the conduct of firms, but they influence the institutions that do. They facilitate and direct the flow of information, ideas, and influence among the players—both decision-makers and those who seek to influence their decisions. They also provide platforms for the exercise of pressure. Each transnational organization has its own objectives and incentives, and identifying those influences can reveal much about how it exercises its influence. We discuss three that are particularly influential.

ICN (International Competition Network): This organization deals only with competition law.[6] It was created by competition officials from the US, Canada, and others as a forum for exchanging information, experience, and ideas. Its members are CAs, not states. This structure was intended to reduce the influence of politics and lobbyists on competition law development, but it has succeeded in this only to a limited extent. It is a virtual organization—that is, it has no physical location. Annual meetings are held in various parts of the world, but it generally does not provide funding for members to attend, which means that wealthier CAs are more likely to attend the meetings. Moreover, CAs can invite guests from the private sphere to participate (lawyers and economists are often invited) and they have their own agendas. Much of the ICN's work is done in working groups that deal with specific issues through electronic means. Each member may invite "specialists"—lawyers and economists—to attend and participate, and often they influence discussions. Some working groups

---

[6] International Competition Network, 'About the ICN' (*International Competition Network*) <https://www.internationalcompetitionnetwork.org/about/> accessed November 4, 2019.

issue "recommended practices." A few of these have been widely accepted—primarily those involving procedural standardization. It is important to recognize, however, that such recommendations represent various levels of support among the members.

OECD (Organisation for Economic Co-operation and Development): This Paris-based organization is highly influential in many areas of economic policy.[7] Members are states, and membership is often viewed as a mark of achievement—entry into an elite circle which can bring rewards to both states and their representatives. The members generally include wealthier, more stable, and more democratic states, and the organization inevitably tends to represent their interests. A state's influence within the organization reflects its political and economic influence as well as its financial contributions to the organization. The general status and importance of the OECD also supports its role and influence in the global competition law system.

The organization contains a large and active competition section. The staff includes highly reputed economists, and not surprisingly they tend to promote the role of economics in competition law. The section often hosts conferences and discussions, some of which include non-member participants. Its representatives participate in and influence competition law discussions around the world. These provide a platform that channels the flow of pressures, information, and ideas among competition officials and scholars from both member and non-member countries.

UNCTAD (UN Commission on Trade and Development): The competition organ of the UN reflects the structure of the UN membership and therefore pays particular attention to the interests of emerging market states.[8] This leads to a focus on developmental goals that are important in those states (see Ch. 10) including social and political goals. The office is smaller than the OECD's competition group, and it can be hampered by the

---

[7] Organisation for Economic Co-operation and Development, 'Who We Are' (*Organisation for Economic Co-Operation and Developing*) <https://www.oecd.org/about/> accessed November 4, 2019.

[8] United Nations Conference on Trade and Development, 'Themes' (*United Nations Conference on Trade and Development*) <https://unctad.org/en/Pages/themes.aspx> accessed November 4, 2019.

cumbersome bureaucracy of the UN, but leading figures in it are sometimes highly influential among CAs in emerging markets and beyond.

CUTS International (Consumer Unity & Trust Society): This is a transnational organization that focuses on the trade, competition law, and development issues of emerging market countries.[9] Headquartered in India, it also has offices in the US and elsewhere. It makes competition policy recommendations, particularly in relation to issues of trade and economic development. It is also very prominent online—often presenting information and opinions on trade and competition law issues. Finally, it holds conferences on global competition law issues that are increasingly attended by both representatives of emerging market economies and those who want to understand more about decision making in such countries.

c. Secondary players

Lobbyists, lawyers, economists, accountants, and management consultants all influence competition law decisions—sometimes strongly, so their roles are an integral part of the global system. Large law firms and management consultancy firms, for example, now operate in many countries and spread their messages throughout the areas in which they are active. They create webs of relationships in which competition law officials from multiple states are often included.

Their principal objectives are to influence competition agencies (and sometimes courts and legislatures) to make decisions that favor their clients. They are paid to lobby on behalf of their clients (or to perform other services for them) so their primary objective is to secure the outcomes that their clients hire them to achieve. They may also have intra-professional objectives that are worth noting. All professionals have reason to promote the role of their profession and thereby increase their own status and earning potential. For example, economists have incentives to foster the use

---

[9] Consumer Unity & Trust Society, 'Who We Are' (*Consumer Unity & Trust Society*) <https://cuts-international.org/who-we-are/> accessed November 4, 2019.

of economics in competition law, because the more economics is used, the more status economists have and the greater their potential earnings may be. Lawyers from countries with significant experience in using economics for these purposes have similar incentives to promote its use. Lawyers that do not have such experience generally promote reliance on more traditional methods and objectives.

In some regimes, legal and economic academic "experts" play important and constructive roles. They provide opinions to CAs, legislatures, and sometimes courts. Some institutions pay them directly. This provides incentives for them to remain (or at least appear) impartial and objective. In others they are paid by clients to serve the client's interests. Some are university professors who may seek to influence other members of their respective professions as well as government decision-makers. Others have achieved expertise in practice and may be driven by more private incentives. It is often useful to pay careful attention to how experts are chosen and compensated and to their incentives in providing their opinions to public officials.

General influence flows: The vast river of information, ideas, and opinions about and involving competition law that circulate on the internet also influences competition law decisions. But how? Basically, each individual and institution pays attention to some items and neglects others, valuing some more highly than others on the basis of its own incentives and objectives. Domestic factors are inevitably important in these assessments, because they often provide the most recognizable and immediate benefits to the decision-makers, but the global system itself also arranges and shapes perceptions and incentives.

Networks of relationships are often particularly influential in shaping what an individual or institution attends to on the internet. These networks are usually based on shared interests and perceptions of benefit. Those who share particular concerns, interests, or ideologies tend to look at the same information and interpret it in similar ways. For example, those who seek to become members of the OECD may pay particular attention to the information the OECD presents on its website, what the representatives of the OECD say and write, what others write and say about their entry into the organization, and so on. As noted earlier, membership in the organization provides many benefits and tends to be highly sought after. Ideologies can have similar influence on network formation and operation, because they are often widely shared. Knowing how they are shared across the institutions and decision-makers in the global system points to information and factors that we might not otherwise see.

These network factors also help us to make sense of convergence issues, which have been a central theme in competition law discussions since the 1990s. For most of that period, competition laws around the world appeared to be converging toward a more economics-based model of competition law as was being promoted by the US.[10] This put pressure on decision-makers to conform to that model, which some have seen as an "international standard." Recognizing the development of a global adaptive system reveals that this view of convergence is too simple. The cross-cutting relationships within that system influence decisions in many ways. This may lead to convergence in some areas and divergence in others, but both are likely to change as new factors influence the system. The rise of Big Data that we discuss in the next chapter provides good examples.

This chapter has highlighted the interactions among competition law players and the global system that shapes them and is shaped by them. It has shown how the individual institutions and influences discussed in earlier chapters flow together in streams within this system. Recognizing how the system functions provides a powerful lens for penetrating the mass of details about competition law across the globe and provides insights into decisions throughout the system.

The next and last chapter identifies two of the main changes facing competition law, examines the challenges they represent for public officials and practitioners, and notes some of the responses to them.

---

[10] David J. Gerber, *Global Competition: Law, Markets, and Globalization* (2010) *esp. Ch. 8.*

12

CHALLENGES AND CHANGES

Competition law's task is to reduce restraints on competition, so those who apply it must understand the *kind of competition* to which they are applying it. As we have seen, in recent decades competition law has focused on competition based on prices (and factors that influence prices) but digitalization and globalization have created new forms and dimensions of economic competition, and competition law institutions must address and respond to the changes. When they do not, decision-makers misunderstand the consequences of conduct; advisers give poor advice; and lawyers, economists, and others may not adequately protect their clients' interests. This chapter identifies these changes and the challenges they pose for competition law, notes some of their consequences, and outlines responses. As always, the Guide focuses on the essentials of these issues so that you can recognize what you need to know without being burdened by unhelpful and misleading information.

The chapter focuses on two profound and lasting changes in competition. One is the deepening and widening of globalization, which alters the *dimensions of markets*; the other is the digital economy, which creates new *forms of competition*. Together, they challenge both domestic regimes and the global system.

The chapter has three main objectives: (1) to identify the challenges and some of their impacts; (2) to note how individual regimes are responding to these changes; (3) and to identify key factors that shape their responses.

A. DEEP GLOBALIZATION: CHANGING COMPETITION'S DIMENSIONS

The deepening and broadening of economic globalization alters the dimensions of competition by reducing location-based barriers

Competition Law and Antitrust. David J. Gerber, Oxford University Press (2020). © David J. Gerber.
DOI: 10.1093/oso/9780198727477.001.0001

to competition. The basic process is not new, but its extent and depth are! Competition now involves more decision-makers making a broader range of decisions among more alternatives and with potentially greater and more complex effects on society. In short, it creates more complex and interrelated transnational environments for competition. This is "deep globalization."

Here are some of the key changes that are relevant to competition law:

1. Deep globalization expands more markets across state boundaries, often altering in the process the economic functions they perform and the interests they affect.

2. It intertwines cross-border markets and societies in more ways and more tightly. The dramatic increase in the number and extent of global supply chains is a prominent example. These arrangements often relate numerous firms across many national boundaries. The many contractual and managerial ties among the parties have consequences for economic, political, and social interests in each one. They also often generate cross-boundary struggles over power within the chains themselves.

3. Expanding markets often increase the concentration of wealth and power in the hands of those with the resources and opportunities to take advantage of the opportunities those markets create.

4. These larger markets can facilitate development in emerging markets, creating new opportunities for those who otherwise would have fewer opportunities to sell their goods and service or otherwise advance their interests. Yet they can also skew economic development to serve the interests of larger and richer firms which are centered outside emerging market countries.

5. This phase of globalization also tends to expand the roles of foreign players in domestic economic decisions. Increasing contractual and property relations across borders creates opportunities for multiple economic, legal, and political actors outside a country to exert influences within it. The growing complexity of business–government relationships magnifies these effects.

6. The broadening dimensions of competition increase the uncertainty of market relations. Who owns what? Who is involved in what? Who has power where and how and over what? Who is exerting influence on which decisions?

7. The political dimensions of these changes can buffet competition law. In many emerging market economies, for example, they intensify domestic awareness of the degree to which foreign firms and governments control their destinies, leading to resentment and pressures on competition law to control their influence. For example, some see the changes as a reason for demanding greater concern for fairness in competition law.

B. THE DIGITAL ECONOMY: NEW FORMS OF COMPETITION

Digital technology modifies existing forms of competition and creates new ones. In traditional markets, firms generally compete by making better products or providing more valuable services at more attractive prices. In this context, a firm or group of firms can subvert competition by acquiring sufficient power over price (or related factors) to be able to act without regard to the constraints of other firms. This power has been the focus of competition law for decades. In the digital economy, however, competitive advantage is not always based on this type of power, but instead on other forms of power that may have similar consequences for competition, so decision-makers must find ways to respond to the threats it poses. This chapter gives a taste of these new developments.

The capacity of computers to acquire, aggregate, encode, manipulate, and strategically deploy very large amounts of information and to perform these functions very quickly is the primary source of change. It enables those who employ the technology to find new forms of market advantage. It often leads them to *compete with and for data*. This is the world of "big data" (BD) and the global digital economy (GDE).

1. NEW TECHNOLOGIES IN TRADITIONAL FORMS OF COMPETITION

Firms can use these new technologies to compete in traditional ways in traditional markets. For example, they can use them to learn more about customers and potential customers by aggregating large amounts of data and identifying patterns in consumer behavior that would otherwise be difficult, if not impossible, to recognize. Here the technology does not change the basic nature of the competition. Instead, it provides additional tools to be used by competing firms, for example, to increase demand for a firm's products or services.

Firms can also extend the reach of traditional strategies by using algorithms to encode and disguise anticompetitive arrangements and conduct. In principle, the technology can even be used to go further and employ artificial intelligence (AI) to identify ways of creating collusion and camouflaging conduct, although this use of AI is fraught with uncertainty and controversy. These uses of technology create new and difficult issues for competition law, but they are essentially elaborations of the basic pattern of competition on traditional markets.

2. NEW FORMS OF COMPETITION

The big change, however, is the use of the technology to create *new forms of competition*! Many of these practices and strategies were not even imaginable before the advent of the digital economy. Their core element is the control of data. In contrast to competition through price or quality, this form of competition is based on the acquisition and manipulation of data. It challenges and often undermines assumptions on which traditional competition law operates.

A firm that controls large amounts of data and uses it more skillfully and strategically than rivals who control less data and/ or use it less skillfully has a significant competitive advantage over them. In this context, skill is based primarily on the quality of the algorithms that the firm employs and the competence and sophistication of those who create and use them.

A central feature of this form of competition is the role of computer platforms. Willing buyers make purchases through a platform that aggregates their requests and directs information about them to sellers. On the other side of the platform, sellers provide their offerings and often pay the platform owners (e.g., Google) for the privilege of using the platform. Any resulting transaction flows over the platform. Information essentially passes through the platform, which through its algorithms shapes the presentation of data to both buyers and sellers. As Amazon and Google users know, this can be a powerful influence on decisions, because it enables the platform rather than the seller to present the relevant data to potential buyers.

In this form of competition, data about buyers becomes itself valuable, and control of data becomes a source of competitive advantage and power. Firms such as Amazon gain economic benefit and power that is based on the number of buyers and sellers who use the platform. Competitors compete with and for data, so firms provide platform services to buyers without charge in order to get their data. This enables the platform owner to charge higher prices for advertising and other forms of access to the buyers represented in the data. In general, the more users a platform has, the greater its value. Platform owners can also use this data to sell their own products or services more effectively, and they can sell the data to others.

3. BIG DATA'S CONTEXT

These uses of digital technology provide significant issues of detection and analysis for competition law institutions, but the "Big" in BD compounds the challenges. This form of competition requires significant investment for acquiring and encoding data, but once acquired the data is not expensive to use, manipulate, and distribute. This front-loaded cost structure fosters "bigness." Within a few years firms such as Google and Amazon became "giants" that dominate their competitive arena. They wield exceptional power not only in economic terms, but also in many other social contexts such as human rights.

Moreover, these dominant firms are geographically concentrated. Most are based in the US. This gives US officials and lawyers experiences and perspectives in competition law that differ from those in most other regimes. These perspectives are associated with those who *own* the platforms. All others *depend on* the platforms, so they often have very different incentives and interests. This is likely to change over time, as firms such as China's Alibaba improve their competitive position, but the first mover advantage of existing BD firms may be difficult to erode.

C. IMPACTS AND RESPONSES: INDIVIDUAL REGIMES

These new forms and dimensions of competition challenge many assumptions and methods of competition law. This section looks at some of the impacts. Recognizing them is essential for understanding where competition law is as well as where it is going.

1. GOALS

The GDE makes it more difficult to know what it means to "deter restraints on competition" which is the central role of competition law. Ideas about what constitutes a restraint in traditional markets are not always applicable in the GDE. In response, some legislatures and Competition Authorities (CAs) modify their stated goals while others rely on reinterpreting existing goals. Uncertainty about goals tends to be greatest where goals are specific—for example, efficiency goals, while broader political and social goals can more easily accommodate change.

Consumer welfare: As noted in Chapter 3, "consumer welfare" is used in several ways in competition law. At its broadest, it signals that competition law is concerned only with effects on consumers and thus excludes political and social factors as goals. When used this way, it can be applied to the GDE with some adjustments. As we noted, however, regimes often use it in a narrower way, using effect on price as the sole or primary measure of consumer welfare—that is, they consider conduct to be anticompetitive when it increases price above a competitive price. Given that prices in digital markets often do not have the same function that they have in traditional markets, however, this price focus may not be useful in identifying harm to competition.

For example, the price for making purchases through a platform is often zero, so there is no price competition.

Economic efficiency and market structure: The changed role of price in the GDE also clouds the value of economic efficiency and market structure goals that rely on price effects.

Innovation and economic development goals are not necessarily based on these price effects, so the GDE may not undermine them. Economic development depends on broader societal and political factors such as education and the role of the government, so the impact of the GDE is less clear. Development economics is itself more contested and less precise than the neo-classical economics that supports price-based goals.

Similarly, the sources of innovation are varied and highly contextual. There are a variety of approaches to these goals, and each rests on assumptions about how the goals can be achieved and therefore about the kind of conduct that is harmful. This makes predictions about their role in the GDE hazardous.

Social/political goals: Goals such as fairness and equality are inherently broader than economic goals, so they are typically less directly affected by the GDE. But BD injects new factors into these goals and thus makes them even more difficult to apply consistently. For example, the power and influence of tech "giants" such as Google can be a critical element in assessing fairness, and widespread public concern over this power also tends to make them attractive political targets.

Privacy as a goal? The GDE generates demands for competition law to include privacy as one of its goals. BD firms often compete with and for personal data. As a result, they may expose personal data to risks that are difficult not only to control, but even to identify. Some argue that competition law must include these goals, primarily because they are inherently tied to competition issues. Others respond that although privacy issues are important, they do not belong in competition law and should be dealt with in other areas of law, notably privacy law or consumer protection law, that are specifically designed to deal with those kinds of issues. For them, including privacy in competition law would undermine the effectiveness of competition law itself while not addressing privacy concerns appropriately. The broader perspective of European competition law has generally given greater weight to privacy goals than has the narrower perspective of economic analysis that animates US antitrust. Many competition law regimes do not have the resources to consider the issues carefully, so they look to the major players for guidance.

2. METHODS

The BDE also challenges some competition law methods. Methods can only provide a reliable path to goals if those applying the methods have a sound basis for predicting the consequences of applying the methods. As we have seen, however, the GDE makes the consequences of conduct more difficult to assess. Would breaking up large tech companies or limiting their capacity to expand have positive effects on competition? No one can be confident of the answer.

Power is central to competition law analysis, because it *enables firms to restrain competition*. Power in the digital economy often rests on how much data a firm controls, and tools have not yet been developed to analyze such power or assess its impact.

Economic methods: Economic methods have evolved to assess power in relation to price, and they have become convincing in doing that. But relying on price to signal power where competition is not based on price can be both misleading and harmful. As we have seen, power in digital markets is often based on control of data, and few would claim that economic science has developed a clear understanding of its contours and of the ways in which it can be used. Economics will eventually evolve to analyze this new form of power effectively, but this may take decades as theories are developed and tested. Moreover, the resulting methods may be more complex and thus less suitable for use by legal institutions.

Standard legal methods: The GDE also presents obstacles to the effective use of standard legal methods such as statutory interpretation and case analysis. For example, the interpretation of fixed texts such as statutes and guidelines is convincing only when it is based on a shared sense of the meaning of the language used in the text. Language intended to apply to competition in traditional markets (e.g., predatory pricing—reducing prices to drive out competitors) makes little sense if applied to digital markets in which prices are zero. This leads to uncertainty in applying the language to a digital context.

The digital economy raises similar problems for case-based methods. Here decision-makers rely for guidance on earlier cases involving similar situations. Their focus is on comparison of cases. The value of this mechanism is based on the assumption that lessons learned from one fact situation can be applied to others. If, however, a case dealing with a traditional market is applied to a digital market, this assumption may be harmful, because assumptions about the effects of conduct in one may be meaningless when applied to the other. We can again use the role of price as an example: traditional competition law analysis focuses on prices, but in the platform-based markets of the digital economy prices are often zero, making lessons from earlier cases less relevant. Moreover, comparison is valued in part because it can create consistency in applying the law, but if the cases compared refer to fundamentally different forms of competition, comparison can lead instead to the opposite—inconsistency and incoherence.

3. INSTITUTIONS

The GDE not only challenges the capacity of institutions to identify and assess restraints on competition, but it also renders more precarious and more costly their efforts to apply and enforce competition laws. This is particularly likely where the institutions themselves cannot be confident of the methods they use to support their decisions.

Legislatures: Drafting legislation (and other texts such as guidelines) becomes more difficult. Fixed texts use general language to categorize and describe conduct the drafters consider harmful, but if the conduct described in the text is not harmful in a new context such as the digital economy, the language will create confusion and possible harm. This may lead legislatures to use vague language and leave the problems to courts and CAs.

Courts: When making decisions involving the GDE, judges must interpret and apply statutes and cases without confidence that they understand the conduct involved or recognize its likely consequences. They typically have little training in economics and therefore have limited capacity to assess the economic assumptions being applied to digital markets. Many admit that even in traditional contexts competition issues are particularly difficult, and the complexities and newness of the GDE increase this effect. This gives them incentives to resolve cases on procedural rather than substantive grounds.

The incentives to do so are particularly high when courts review administrative decisions. Judges are aware that a CA typically has greater capacity to acquire and analyze factual material than they have. This tends to inhibit courts from overturning CA decisions.

Where courts deal with private enforcement, two additional factors come into play. One is the need to manage the parties' acquisition and presentation of data to the court. The uncertainties surrounding the effects of conduct in the GDE encourage parties to present as much potentially relevant material as possible and to influence its interpretation in any way possible. Where private enforcement relies principally on evidence gathered by public authorities, these incentives can be controlled more easily than in regimes that give litigants broad rights to demand factual material from others and to control its presentation to the court. A second factor relates to disparities in the capacity of parties to pursue claims. Mega-companies that dominate the tech industry can typically deploy far more resources and tap far more digital expertise than litigation opponents who do not have such resources, intensifying perceptions of unfairness.

Competition Authorities: Enforcement agencies often face the greatest challenges. They must make and articulate policies and enforcement decisions—sometimes without a high level of confidence that they fully understand how to classify the conduct or what competitive harm means in the GDE environment. This makes it difficult to achieve defensible, effective enforcement. Moreover, the dynamics of digital markets can change rapidly. Conduct based on a particular power position may be harmful one month but harmless when the power erodes in following months. Competition officials may not learn about these effects until after the power has eroded and the conduct has ceased. As a result, enforcement efforts may have little value or effect.

The GDE also increases the complexity, uncertainty, risks, and costs facing CAs. Some examples:

Acquiring information: Although technology makes information far more plentiful and accessible than in the past, identifying what is worth looking at in the dense thicket of information can be costly and time consuming. Moreover, the tools that provide data can also be used to manipulate and camouflage that data, enabling sophisticated tech managers to create obstacles to a CA's inquiry into what is actually happening.

Support and compliance: The GDE may impair support for the CA's activities. It may, for example, erode domestic support for competition law. In many countries, there is limited willingness to invest scarce resources in competition law because there is little confidence that it will provide benefits that justify its costs. Where the GDE increases uncertainty about the nature and effects of competition, it also increases that skepticism. This can reduce political and financial support for a CA and undermine its effectiveness in investigating and assessing conduct and in retaining high quality officials. In addition, high tech global firms command extensive resources and important political connections, and they have strong incentives to use them to the fullest to combat enforcement efforts. For example, officials in many newer CAs have relatively low wages, so the prospect of external rewards (potentially including graft) is likely to be attractive. This can inhibit enforcement against the firms that are the source of these rewards.

But digital technology can also aid enforcement for those CAs that can afford to use it. They can use it, for example, to detect potentially anticompetitive conduct by identifying patterns in price movements that might be evidence of coordinated conduct and that might not otherwise be noted. They can also use it to monitor the conduct of specific firms in order to develop a clearer picture of what the objectives of management are as well as of the effects of the conduct.

4. TARGETS

These factors influence competition law's targets. A few examples:

Horizontal agreements: The GDE can make cartels more difficult to detect. For example, globalization facilitates collusion in locations that are difficult to monitor—deals arranged on a golf course in Myanmar are not easily detected, and technology provides new ways for competitors to coordinate their conduct that are more difficult to detect. Signaling information can be encoded on websites and digital exchanges in numerous ways, and a CA may have little or no capacity to recognize or follow the signals. On the other hand, technology also provides more advanced tools for detecting collusion, although not all CAs can afford them. Moreover, businesses seeking to avoid the law's reach are typically more adept at using them than government officials, and their incentives for doing so can be very strong.

Vertical agreements: Assessing the impact of vertical agreements on competition is difficult even in traditional markets, as we have seen, but the GDE adds complexity and uncertainty. The increased geographical reach, complexity, and technological sophistication of both supply and marketing relations can significantly increase the difficulty and costs of identifying anticompetitive effects. Moreover, the digital economy's emphasis on speed of innovation strengthens claims that "too much intervention" can impede economic development and harm not only industries, but communities and national economies. Finally, the digital technology's capacity to tailor marketing and pricing to individual consumers increases the potential harms from the anticompetitive effects of discriminating among purchasers.

Unilateral conduct: As we have seen (Ch. 6) identifying harm from unilateral conduct is often challenging, primarily because there is no specific event such as an agreement that calls attention to it. The conduct is also embedded in the business plan of a single firm, making it hard to isolate from other elements in the plan. The complexity and expanse of GDE markets make both obstacles more formidable. Moreover, heightened political sensitivity to the power of large tech companies often translates into increased demands to increase enforcement in this area despite the difficulty of finding or developing legal principles to support enforcement decisions. This tends to undermine confidence in the legal basis for enforcement. Smaller CAs in emerging markets often face particularly strong political sensitivity to the power of foreign tech firms, but limited resources and technical skills can hamper their capacity to respond to these firms.

Mergers: These factors weigh heavily on merger control, primarily because it *requires predicting the probable effects* of a merger.

Rapid evolution of global economic relations makes the definition of markets more precarious, and the often tectonic changes
in technology make predicting the effects of mergers in those
markets a daunting and uncertain task.

D. IMPACTS AND RESPONSES: THE GLOBAL SYSTEM

The GDE impacts not only individual regimes, but also the global
system—its composition and its dynamics. Recall that the system
is adaptive and interactive. It responds to external factors such as
deep globalization, which increases the number and diversity of
players, and technology, which reconfigures what the players do
and how they do it.

1. PLAYERS

States: The new entrants into the global arena are more diverse
in their interests, resources, and capacities than the small circle of
industrialized countries that has been the center of the competition law universe since its beginnings. They often face obstacles
that were rarely if ever faced in Europe, the US, or Japan—for
example, deep-seated and extensive corruption, lack of resources,
low levels of economic sophistication, and many others. Digital
technology adds new pressures and incentives to these obstacles.
Perhaps the most powerful of these is the fact that the leaders of
the tech world are located in a small number of countries, notably
the US. These countries and institutions gain from the power and
influence of the firms located there; other countries use their
services, but they are often wary of depending on them.

Transnational organizations: The GDE also impacts the role
of transnational organizations. For example, the growing complexity of the competition law environment increases their potential value as platforms for sharing experience and expertise. It
also tends to shift attention to technology concerns, which can be
particularly valuable for those in newer institutions or with limited resources who may not have the funds to assess these factors
themselves. On the other hand, that complexity may make it
difficult for a transnational organization to make its policies and

suggestions clear and convincing. Moreover, the increased diversity of interests and circumstances among competition law's players makes it more difficult to claim that a particular policy fits all needs. In that sense, the organizations may have more difficulty playing the role of "purveyors of truth."

Secondary players: Globalization increases the number and variety of private groups and institutions that can influence competition law decisions, and technology generates new roles and capacities for them. This combination inevitably brings additional burdens for CAs, who must respond to these efforts. Yet it can also benefit them by providing them with additional information and more transnational connections that can aid their detection and enforcement efforts.

Central to this development is the growth in number and influence of very large and institutionally powerful firms of lawyers, management consultants, economists, and others. Many operate throughout the competition law world. Their services are valued by firms that operate on a transnational scale, because they internalize, organize, and share information about many countries, institutions, and markets. These firms have their own agendas and objectives, of course, and they often devote extensive resources to influencing competition law decisions. Moreover, they can use their contacts in many parts of the world to coordinate their efforts and increase their influence. Efforts to convince one set of decision-makers (e.g., in Japan, Brazil, or Chile) may be enhanced by successes in convincing others (e.g., in Brussels).

Large global law firms are at the center of this evolution. They offer globally integrated legal services that can be of much value, especially for large, multinational companies. This global integration of legal services has parallels among management consultants and accountants, and it has contributed to the blending together of these formerly independent professional groups. In many countries, legal and professional rules and customs keep the two professions separate, but they are typically interwoven for global operations.

Economists have followed the trend, although they seldom produce such large-scale operations. They have uniquely valuable tools for grasping the impact of global markets, so they become increasingly influential and powerful as global competition

expands and becomes more complex. In addition, many competition law regimes give increasing weight to economics at both
policy and enforcement levels. Finally, the digital economy
creates a new and often highly influential professional group of
digital technology specialists who often work with economists.
They are indispensable for CAs trying to develop tools for use
in digital markets. The benefits that these organizations provide
are, however, often available at prices that only large businesses
can afford.

Other lobbying groups also influence decisions within the
system. These include, for example, organizations that represent
the interests of specific industries (e.g., steel or car manufacturing).
Similarly, labor groups have influential voices in some countries
and groups of countries. Technological globalization enables these
groups to cooperate with each other across national boundaries,
and thereby enhance their influence.

2. INTERACTIONS

The GDE also reconfigures relations and interactions among
competition law regimes.

Knowing the other players: It increases the availability of some
types of information about other regimes, although the information is not always as useful as it might seem. For example, it
often includes extensive data about specific actions of a CA or the
number of its employees, but it less often provides information
about the CA's informal actions and other factors that influence
decisions (see Ch. 10). Sometimes knowing about these influences
has more practical importance than the results of specific cases,
which may be of limited value in interpreting past decisions or
predicting what a CA is likely to do in the GDE environment.
Moreover, technology can also be used to manipulate information and thereby distort images of the players.

Shared content: Digital technology enhances the importance
of shared content in the competition law arena. For example,
it makes available competition law models such as those developed by the OECD and other transnational organizations. These
are used as common points of reference by all organizations and
individuals, promoting dialogue and facilitating communication

among them. Yet other forms of shared content can have the opposite effect. The almost limitless amounts of information available about specific actions and the abundance of claims by varying groups and institutions can easily lead to uncertainty and confusion and thus a weaker basis for agreement and understanding.

Communicating: Issues common to digital communication in general—fast connections, vulnerability to manipulation etc.—have more specific effects in the context of communicating about competition law. For example, communication must usually be in the English language, but participants differ significantly in their English language capabilities. A non-native speaker may, for example, use a term from US antitrust law to refer to a legal concept or institution that seems to the speaker to be appropriate, but s/he may use the term in way that differs in important ways from the way it is used in the US, and others may not be aware of the discrepancy. "Discovery" might be an example. It is often used by foreign observers to refer merely to a court's acquisition of evidence, but in US legal usage it refers to a very specific procedural mechanism in which lawyers acquire information and to which many rules and interpretations are attached. This kind of misunderstanding can lead to serious mistakes and undermine confidence in communication. Moreover, as we have noted, competition law is not a "natural" form of law (e.g., in contrast to criminal law or contracts). It must be constructed by statute and developed and applied by domestic institutions. This increases the likelihood that others from other regimes will not be aware of the meanings attached to the words used or the functions and roles of the institutions that use them. Finally, digital communication is highly compressed. The lack of context can make it difficult to discover and clarify underlying differences.

Converging? Diverging? Coordinating? The GDE also impacts convergence issues. On the one hand, shared information and models expand the potential for convergence. Models can frame and concentrate convergence efforts, and increased information about the actions and statements of other players enables decision-makers to identify those who may have similar interests in a particular area or issue, further supporting convergence. These factors have generated widespread convergence in a few areas, notably procedural issues such as the requirements for merger notifications. They have also increased similarities in the use of methods, particularly economic methods. As we have seen, however, the GDE can lead to increases rather than decreases in differences among systems. Those who dominate the GDE—for example, large tech firms and the governments that host them—may pursue goals and methods that differ from those who have less power and influence in that arena.

Similar effects confront efforts to increase coordination and cooperation among competition law systems. The increased number of participants in the system as well as the diversity of their interests and the contexts in which they operate increase the potential value of coordination, but they also make coordination more difficult.

★★★

Deep globalization and the digital economy combine to challenge competition law—not only the intellectual and practical capacity of institutions to comprehend and respond effectively to the challenges they present, but also the political support for those efforts. The key question for the future: is this a brave new world or do we simply need to refine the tools. Stay tuned!

NOTES ON USING THE GUIDE

This is a new kind of guide, so I offer here a few suggestions for using it.

Goals: Keep the Guide's goals in mind! They explain why information is included or excluded and why materials are presented the way they are. The central goal is to open doors to competition law in both its domestic and global dimensions—for both those who are new to it and those who want to know more about some aspect of it. This requires a broad view that highlights relationships between the domestic and global dimensions of competition law. Recognizing how the national relates to the global is central to understanding and functioning in competition law in the digital age.

Context: The Guide is designed for a new context, and that shapes what the Guide does and how it does it. The central features of this context are: (1) the increasingly transnational scope of markets and the complexity of competition on those markets; (2) the large and growing number of diverse individuals and institutions who are either involved with competition law or influence competition law decisions; (3) the extensive and almost instantaneous connection of these participants through digital technology; and (4) the fact that potentially relevant information is massive, dense, immediate, and highly manipulable.

Skills: The Guide emphasizes several skills as keys to operating in this new environment.

1. *Recognizing what's happening*: The most fundamental skill is the capacity to make sense of what is happening—that is, to interpret effectively the texts, decisions, and statements that are so abundant in the competition law arena and to see how they relate to and affect each other.

2. *Predicting future decisions*: Decision-makers in law almost always use the past in predicting the future. Will s/he use her authority in ways I want or ways I fear? This is what clients pay lawyers, consultants, and economists to do, and it is usually what analysts in and out of government want to know. The GDE adds new complexity to making these

predictions. The Guide is specifically designed to improve
the capacity to make the needed predictions.

3. *Communicating*: Skill in communicating with others in
the global system is central to both understanding and
predicting. The capacity to understand what is happening
depends on the ability to acquire and evaluate information
from others; the capacity to predict what is likely to happen
depends on the ability to grasp the messages that often
lie undetected in available materials; and the capacity to
influence outcomes depends on the ability to recognize
what others see, mean, want, and expect.

Tools and strategies: The Guide uses three main tools to support
and develop these skills.

1. *Focus on decisions*: Each of the skills depends on the
capacity to recognize the factors that are likely to
influence decisions, so the Guide focuses on decisions
and the influences that shape them. Each decision has a
specific location within the global arena. An individual or
institution makes a decision—whether formal or informal
or concealed—in a specific context. Focusing on the
decision requires that we ask who is making it and where
the individual or institution is located in the global system.
This then helps to identify the influences on it. It is a
powerful tool for separating valuable information from the
abundance of other available information. It sharpens our
capacity to interpret what has happened, to predict what
is likely to happen, and to communicate effectively about
competition law issues.

2. *Focus on system*: Decisions are shaped by the institutions
and individuals that make them, so we need to recognize
how institutions and individuals relate to each other. The
Guide explains how competition law decision-makers
interact to form the global competition law system, and it
shows how that system functions and exerts its influence.

3. *Chunking*: The technique of condensing or "chunking"
information is particularly valuable for using these tools.
Large amounts of information provide the material for
performing the tasks we want to perform, but they can
overwhelm our capacity to grasp what is relevant. This

requires a leaner approach to information than was used in pre-digital times, so the Guide clarifies the picture by recognizing patterns in the data, identifying core elements that are widely shared, and noting variations on those themes.

Framework: Keeping the Guide's overall structure in mind helps to clarify the ways in which information and insights are related. The Guide first provides a *core definition* of competition law that can be used in any regime, together with a preliminary review of how systems vary. This is a necessary basis for any discussion of competition law. It then identifies the spectrum of *goals* that competition law regimes use in making decisions and the various *methods* that lead from goals to decisions. *Institutions* use these methods, so the Guide looks at how they use them and at the factors that shape their efforts. Methods, institutions, and goals determine the targets of competition law, so Chapters 5–7 look at what these *targets* are, why they are seen as harmful, and the factors that influence enforcement against them. In order to understand how the global system functions and identify important influences at both the domestic and global levels, the Guide devotes individual chapters to the competition law regimes of the *US* and the *EU*, and it then highlights the *factors that shape all competition laws* and that therefore can be used to better understand any regime. The following chapter ties many of these elements together by showing how the institutions, players, and interest function together to create an interactive *global system*. The last chapter looks at the *challenges* facing competition law, especially digitization and digital markets.

The Guide is designed for use by anyone who wants to better understand competition law—whether student, practicing lawyer, government official, business person, scholar, or any other reader interested in global economic developments. Each can use it to achieve desired objectives. I am confident that all can benefit.

READING LISTS

CHAPTER 2 WHAT IS IT? COMPETITION LAW'S VEILED IDENTITY

- Phillip E. Areeda and Herbert Hovenkamp, *Fundamentals of Antitrust Law* (4th ed., 2011)
- Jonathan B. Baker, *The Antitrust Paradigm: Restoring a Competitive Economy* (2019)
- Daniel A. Crane and Herbert Hovenkamp, *The Making of Competition Policy: Legal and Economic Resources* (2013)
- Vinod Dhall, *Competition Law Today: Concepts, Issues and the Law in Practice* (2nd ed., 2019)
- David J. Gerber, "Comparative Antitrust Law" in Mathias Reimann and Reinhard Zimmerman (eds.), *Oxford Handbook of Comparative Law* (3rd ed., 2019)
- John E. Kwoka Jr. and Lawrence J. White, *The Antitrust Revolution: Economics, Competition, and Policy* (5th ed., 2009)
- Massimo Motta, *Competition Policy: Theory and Practice* (2004)
- Richard A. Posner, *Antitrust Law* (2d ed., 2019)
- Edwin Rockefeller, *The Antitrust Religion* (2007)
- Richard Whish and David Bailey, *Competition Law* (9th ed., 2018)

CHAPTER 3 THE GOALS AND USES OF COMPETITION LAW

- Jonathan B. Baker, "Economics and Politics: Perspectives on the Goals and Future of Antitrust," *Fordham Law Review* Volume 81, page 2175 (2013)
- Robert Bork, *The Antitrust Paradox* (1978)
- Daniel Crane, "The Tempting of Antitrust: Robert Bork and the Goals of Antitrust Policy," *Antitrust Law Journal* Volume 79, page 835 (2014)
- Josef Drexl et al., *Competition Policy and the Economic Approach* (2001)
- Josef Drexl, Laurence Idot, and Joel Moneger, *Economic Theory and Competition Law* (2001)

- Ariel Ezrachi, "'Sponge,'" *Journal of Antitrust Enforcement* Volume 5, page 49 (2017)
- William Kovacic and Ben van Rompuy, *Economic Efficiency: The Sole Concern of Modern Antitrust Policy?: Non-Efficiency Considerations under Article 101 TFEU* (2012)
- Robert H. Lande, "A Traditional and Textualist Analysis of the Goals of Antitrust: Efficiency, Preventing Theft from Consumers, and Consumer Choice," *Fordham Law Review* Volume 81, page 2349 (2013)
- George K. Lipimile, "Competition Policy as Stimulus for Enterprise Development" in UNCTAD, *Competition, Competitiveness and Development: Lessons from Developing Countries* (UNCTAD/DITC/CLP/2004/1, Geneva, 2004) <http://www.unctad.org/en/docs/ditcclp20041ch3_en.pdf>
- Maurice E. Stucke, "Reconsidering Antitrust's Goals," *Boston College Law Review* Volume 53, page 551 (2012)
- Daniel Zimmer (ed.), *The Goals of Competition Law* (2012)

CHAPTER 4 INSTITUTIONS AND METHODS: IMPLEMENTING COMPETITION LAW GOALS

- Oliver Budzinski, "International Antitrust Institutions," in Roger D. Blair and D. Daniel Sokol (eds.), *The Oxford Handbook of International Antitrust Economics*, Volume I, pages 119–46 (2015)
- Daniel A. Crane, *The Institutional Structure of Antitrust Enforcement* (2011)
- Eleanor M. Fox, "Antitrust and Institutions: Design and Change," *Loyola University of Chicago Law Journal* Volume 41, page 473 (2010)
- Eleanor M. Fox and Michael J. Trebilcock, *The Design of Competition Law Institutions: Global Norms, Local Choices* (2013)
- David J. Gerber, "Competition Law and the Institutional Embeddedness of Economics," in Josef Drexl et al. (eds.), *Economic Theory and Competition Law* pages 20–45 (2009)
- William E. Kovacic, "Achieving Better Practices in the Design of Competition Policy Institutions," *Antitrust Bulletin* Volume 50, page 511 (2005)
- D. Daniel Sokol, "Monopolists Without Borders: The Institutional Challenge of International Antitrust in a Global Gilded Age," *Berkeley Business Law Journal* Volume 4, page 37 (2007)

- Javier Tapia and Santiago Montt, "Judicial Scrutiny and Competition Authorities: The Institutional Limits on Antitrust," in Ioannis Lianos and D. Daniel Sokol (eds.), *The Global Limits of Competition Law* pages 141–57 (2012)
- Michael J. Trebilcock and Edward M. Iacobucci, "Designing Competition Law Institutions," *World Competition* Volume 25, page 361 (2002)

CHAPTER 5 ANTICOMPETITIVE AGREEMENTS

- Sandra Marco Colino, *Vertical Agreements and Competition Law: A Comparative Study of the EU and US Regimes* (2010)
- Doris Hildebrand, *Economic Analyses of Vertical Agreements: A Self-assessment* (2005)
- Louis Kaplow, "On the Meaning of Horizontal Agreements in Competition Law," *California Law Review* Volume 99, page 683 (2011)
- Valentine Korah, "From Legal Form Toward Economic Efficiency— Article 85(1) of the EEC Treaty in Contrast to U.S. Antitrust," *Antitrust Bulletin* Volume 35, page 1009 (1990)
- Ioannis Lianos and Damien Geradin, "Vertical Agreements," in *Handbook on European Competition Law: Substantive Aspects* (2013)
- Csongor Istvan Nagy, *EU and US Competition Law: Divided in Unity?: The Rule on Restrictive Agreements and Vertical Intra-brand Restraints* (2013)
- Richard Posner, "Vertical Restraints and Antitrust Policy," *University of Chicago Law Review* Volume 72, page 229 (2005)
- Richard Whish and David Bailey, "Horizontal Agreements— Oligopoly, Tacit Collusion and Collective Dominance," in *Competition Law* (7th ed., 2012)
- Frank Wijckmans and Filip Tuytschaever, *"Horizontal Agreements and Cartels" in EU Competition Law* (2015)

CHAPTER 6 DOMINANT FIRM UNILATERAL CONDUCT: MONOPOLIZATION AND ABUSE OF DOMINANCE

- Alden F. Abbott, "A Tale of Two Cities: Brussels, Washington, and the Assessment of Unilateral Conduct," *Antitrust Bulletin* Volume 56, page 103 (2011)
- Mor Bakhoum, "Abuse Without Dominance in Competition Law: Abuse of Economic Dependence and its Interface with Abuse

of Dominance" (Max Planck Institute for Innovation & Competition Research No. 15-15, 2015) <https://ssrn.com/abstract=2703809>

- Einar Elhauge, "Defining Better Monopolization Standards," *Stanford Law Review* Volume 56, page 253 (2003)

- Eleanor M. Fox, "Monopolization, Abuse of Dominance, and the Indeterminacy of Economics: The U.S./E.U. Divide," *Utah Law Review* Volume 2006, page 725 (2006)

- Eleanor M. Fox, "Monopolization and Abuse of Dominance: Why Europe is Different," *Antitrust Bulletin* Volume 59, page 129 (2014)

- Michael S. Gal, "Monopoly Pricing as an Antitrust Offense in the U.S. and the EC: Two Systems of Belief about Monopoly," *Antitrust Bulletin* Volume 49, page 343 (2004)

- Herbert Hovenkamp, Mark D. Janis, and Mark A. Lemley, "Unilateral Refusal to License," *Journal of Competition Law & Economics* Volume 1, page 13 (2006)

- Chiara Fumagalli et al., *Exclusionary Practices: The Economics of Monopolisation and Abuse of Dominance* (2018)

- Mark Furse, "Excessive Prices, Unfair Prices and Economic Value: The Law of Excessive Pricing under Article 82 EC and the Chapter II Prohibition," *European Competition Journal* Volume 4, page 59 (2008)

- David J. Gerber, "The Future of Article 82: Dissecting the Conflict," in ClausDieter Ehlermann and Mel Marquis (eds.), *European Competition Law Annual 2007* (2008)

- Thomas Krattenmaker and Steven C. Salop, "Anticompetitive Exclusion: Rising Rivals' Costs to Achieve Power Over Price," *Yale Law Journal* Volume 96, page 209 (1986)

- William E. Kovacic, "The Intellectual DNA of Modern U.S. Competition Law for Dominant Firm Conduct: The Chicago/ Harvard Double Helix," *Columbia Business Law Review* Volume 1, page 1 (2007)

- Mark-Oliver Mackenrodt, Beatriz Conde Gallego, and Stefan Enchelmaier, *Abuse of Dominant Position: New Interpretations, New Enforcement Mechanisms?* (2008)

- Tadashi Shiraishi, "A Baseline for Analyzing Exploitative Abuse of a Dominant/Superior Position" (March 1, 2013) <https://ssrn.com/abstract=2246558>

- Sayako Takizawa and Koki Arai, "Abuse of Superior Bargaining Position: the Japanese Experience," *Journal of European Competition Law & Practice* Volume 5, page 8 (2014)

- David J. Teece and Mary Coleman, "The Meaning of Monopoly: Antitrust Analysis in High Technology Industries," *Antitrust Bulletin* Volume 43, page 801 (1998)

CHAPTER 7 MERGERS AND ACQUISITIONS

- Oliver Budzinski, "Toward an International Governance of Transborder Mergers? Competition Networks and Institutions Between Centralism and Decentralism," *New York University Journal of International Law and Politics* Volume 36, Issue 1, page 36 (2003)

- Herbert Hovenkamp and Robert Bork, "Vertical Integration: Leverage, Foreclosure, and Efficiency," *Antitrust Law Journal* Volume 79, page 983 (2014)

- Michael L. Katz and Howard A. Shelanski, "Mergers and Innovation," *Antitrust Law Journal* Volume 74, Issue 1, page 537 (2007)

- William E. Kovacic, Petros C. Mavroidis, and Damien Neven, *Merger Control Procedures and Institutions: A Comparison of the EU and US Practice* (2014)

- John Kwoka, *Mergers, Merger Control, and Remedies: A Retrospective Analysis of U.S. Policy* (2015)

- Michael Porter, "Competition and Antitrust: Towards a Productive-Based Approach to Evaluating Mergers and Joint Ventures," in *Perspectives on Fundamental Antitrust Theory* (2001)

- Michael H. Riordan and Steven C. Salop, "Evaluating Vertical Mergers: A Post-Chicago Approach," *Antitrust Law Journal* Volume 63, page 513 (1995)

- Stephen Salop, "Invigorating Vertical Merger Enforcement," *Yale Law Journal* Volume 127, page 1962 (2018)

CHAPTER 8 US ANTITRUST LAW: CENTRAL, BUT UNIQUE

- Marc A. Eisner, *Antitrust and the Triumph of Economics* (1991)

- Eleanor M. Fox, "The Modernization of Antitrust: A New Equilibrium," *Cornell Law Review* Volume 66, page 1140 (1991)

- Andrew I. Gavil and Harry First, *The Microsoft Antitrust Cases* (2014)

- David J. Gerber, "U.S. Antitrust Law and the Convergence of Competition Laws," reprinted in Jurgen Basedow (ed.), *Limits and Control of Competition with a View to International Harmonization* (2003)
- Herbert Hovenkamp, *Enterprise and American Law, 1836–1937* (1991)
- Herbert Hovenkamp, *The Antitrust Enterprise: Principle and Execution* (2005)
- Robert A. Katzmann, *Regulatory Bureaucracy: The Federal Trade Commission and Antitrust Policy* (1980)
- William E. Kovacic, *Evolution of U.S. Antitrust Enforcement* (2011)
- Mark A. Lemley and Christopher R. Leslie, "Categorical Analysis in Antitrust Jurisprudence," *Iowa Law Review* Volume 93, page 1207 (2008)
- William Letwin, *Law and Economic Policy in America: The Evolution of the Sherman Antitrust Act* (1981)
- William H. Page, "Legal Realism and the Shaping of Modern Antitrust," *Emory Law Journal* Volume 44, Issue 1, page 51 (1995)
- Rudolph Peritz, *Competition Policy in America 1888–1992* (1996)

CHAPTER 9 COMPETITION LAW IN EUROPE

- Oles Andriychuk, *The Normative Foundations of European Competition Law* (2017)
- David Bailey and Laura Elizabeth John, *Bellamy & Child: European Union Law of Competition* (2019)
- Pablo Ibáñez Colomo, *The Shaping of EU Competition Law* (2018)
- Alison Jones and Brenda Sufrin, *EU Competition Law: Text, Cases, and Materials* (6th ed., 2016)
- Ariel Ezrachi, *EU Competition Law: An Analytical Guide to the Leading Cases* (6th ed., 2018)
- Ian Forrester, "Modernization of EC Competition Law," *Fordham International Law Journal* Volume 23, page 1028 (2000)
- David J. Gerber, *Law and Competition in Twentieth Century Europe: Protecting Prometheus* (1998)
- David J. Gerber, "Two Forms of Modernization in European Competition Law," *Fordham International Law Journal* Volume 31, page 1235 (2008)
- Kai Hüschelrath and Heike Schweitzer, *Public and Private Enforcement of Competition Law in Europe: Legal and Economic Perspectives* (2014)

- Ioannis Lianos, Valentine Korah, and Paolo Siciliani, *Competition Law: Analysis, Cases, & Materials* (2019)
- Thomas Mollers and Andreas Heinemann (eds.), *The Enforcement of Competition Law in Europe* (2008)
- Giorgio Monti, *EC Competition Law* (2007)
- Robert O'Donoghue and Jorge Padilla, *The Law and Economics of Article 102 TFEU* (2nd ed., 2013)
- Pier Luigi Parcu, Giorgio Monti, and Marco Botta (eds.), *Abuse of Dominance in EU Competition Law: Emerging Trends* (2017)
- Weijer VerLoren Van Themaat and Berend Reuder, *European Competition Law: A Case Commentary* (2nd ed., 2018)
- Frank Wijckmans and Filip Tuytschaever, *Horizontal Agreements and Cartels in EU Competition Law* (2015)

CHAPTER 10 OTHER COMPETITION LAWS: SHAPING FACTORS

- Michal Gal, *Competition Policy for Small Market Economies* (2003)
- David Lewis (ed.), *Building New Competition Law Regimes* (2013)
- Erlinda M. Medalla, *Competition Policy in East Asia* (2005)
- Richard Whish and Christopher Townley (eds.), *New Competition Jurisdictions: Shaping Policies and Building Institutions* (2012)

CHINA:

- David J. Gerber, "Economics, Law and Institutions: The Development of Competition Law in China," *Washington University Journal of Law & Policy* Volume 26, page 271 (2008)
- Wendy Ng, *The Political Economy of Competition Law in China* (2018)
- Xiaoye Wang, *The Evolution of Chinese Antimonopoly Law* (2019)
- Tingting Weinreich-Zhao, *Chinese Merger Control Law: An Assessment of its Competition-Policy Orientation after the First Years of Application* (2014)
- Mark Williams, *Competition Policy and Law in China, Hong Kong and Taiwan* (2005)

JAPAN:

- Koko Arai, *Law and Economics in Japanese Competition Policy* (2019)
- Michael L. Beeman, *Public Policy and Economic Competition in Japan: Change and Continuity in Antimonopoly Policy, 1973–1995* (2002)

- Harry First and Tadashi Shiraishi, "Japan: The Competition Law System and the Country's Norms," in Eleanor M. Fox and Michael J. Trebilcock (eds.), *The Design of Competition Law Institutions: Global Norms, Local Choices* (2013)

- John O. Haley, *Authority Without Power: Law and the Japanese Paradox* (1991)

- Etsuko Kameoka, *Competition Law and Policy in Japan and the EU* (2014)

- Mitsuo Matsushita, *International Trade and Competition Law in Japan* (1993)

- Tadashi Shiraishi, "Customer Location and the International Reach of National Competition Laws," *Japanese Yearbook of International Law* Volume 59, page 202 (2017)

- Masako Wakui, *Antimonopoly Law: Competition Law and Policy in Japan* (2nd ed., 2019)

KOREA:

- Joseph Seon Hur, *Competition Law/Policy and Korean Economic Development* (2004)

- Jung-Won Hyung and Kyung-min Koh, *Competition Law in the Republic of Korea* (2011)

- Oh-Seung Kwon, "Retrospect and Prospect on Korean Antitrust Law," *Journal of Korean Law* Volume 4, page 1 (2005)

- Harry H. Lee, *Competition Law in Korea* (2015)

LATIN AMERICA:

- Claudio Considera and Paulo Correa, "The Political Economy of Antitrust in Brazil: From Price Control to Competition Policy," in Barry E. Hawk (ed.), *Fordham Corporate Law Institute, International Antitrust Law and Policy* (2001)

- Eleanor M. Fox and D. Daniel Sokol, *Competition Law and Policy in Latin America* (2009)

- Alexander Galetovic, *Competition Policy in Chile* (June 2007) <http://papers.ssrn.com/sol3/paper.cfm?abstract_id=1104007>

- Ignacio de León, *Latin American Competition Law and Policy: A Policy in Search of Identity* (2001)

- Ignacio de León, *An Institutional Assessment of Antitrust Policy: The Latin American Experience* (2009)

- Massimo Motta, *Politica de Concorrencia: Teoria e Pratica e Sua Aplicacao no Brasil* (2015)
- Gesner Oliveira and Thomas Fujiwara, "Competition Policy in Developing Economies: The Case of Brazil," *Northwestern Journal of International Law & Business* Volume 26, page 619 (2006)
- Claudia Schatan and Eugenio Rivera Urrutia (eds.), *Competition Policies in Emerging Economies: Lessons and Challenges from Central America and Mexico* (2008)
- R. Shyam and Ana Carrasco-Martin, "The Investment Climate, Competition Policy, and Economic Development in Latin America," *Chicago-Kent Law Review* Volume 83, page 67 (2008)
- "Symposium: The Brazilian Antitrust Regime," *Competition Law International* Volume 1, Issue 1 (2005)

EMERGING MARKETS:

- Josef Drexl et al. (eds.), *Competition Policy and Regional Integration in Developing Countries* (2012)
- Eleanor Fox et al., *Antitrust in Emerging and Developing Countries: Featuring China, India, Mexico Brazil and South Africa* (2015)
- Eleanor M. Fox and Mor Bakhoum, *Making Markets Work for Africa: Markets, Development and Competition Law in Sub-Saharan Africa* (2019)
- David J. Gerber, "Economic Development and Global Competition Law Convergence," in D. Daniel Sokol et al., *Competition Law and Development* (2013)
- Raphael Kaplinsky and Claudia Manning, "Concentration, Competition Policy, and the Role of Small and Medium-sized Enterprises in South Africa's Industrial Development," *The Journal of Development Studies* Volume 35, page 139 (1998)
- Luke Kelly et al., *Principles of Competition Law in South Africa* (2017)
- William E. Kovacic and Marianela Lopez-Galdos, "Lifecycles of Competition Systems: Explaining Variation in the Implementation of New Regimes," *Law & Contemporary Problems* Volume 79, page 85 (2016)
- David Lewis, *Thieves at the Dinner Table: Enforcing the (South African) Competition Act* (2001)
- Hassan Qaqaya and George Lipimile, *The Effects of Anti-Competitive Business Practices on Developing Countries and their Development Prospects* (UNCTAD/DITC/CLP/2008/2, Geneva, 2008) <http://

www.unctad.org/Templates/webflyer.asp?docif-10698& intItemID-4150&lang=1>

- Simon Roberts, "The Role of Competition Policy and Economic Development: The South African Experience," *Development Southern Africa* Volume 21, page 227 (2004)
- A.E. Rodriguez and Ashok Menon, *The Limits of Competition Policy: The Shortcomings of Antitrust in Developing and Reforming Economies* (2010)
- Ajit Singh, *Competition and Competition Policy in Emerging Markets: International and Developmental Dimensions*, UNCTAD Discussion Paper (2002) <http://www.unctad.org/en/docs/ gdsmdpbg2418_en.pdf>
- D. Daniel Sokol, Thomas K. Cheng, and Iannis Lianos, *Competition Law and Development* (2013)

CHAPTER II THE GLOBAL SYSTEM: INTERACTING AND ADAPTING

- Jürgen Basedow (ed.), *Limits and Control of Competition with a View to International Harmonization* (2002)
- Aditya Bhattacharjea, "The Case for a Multilateral Agreement on Competition Policy: A Developing Country Perspective," *Journal of International Economic Law* Volume 9, page 293 (2006)
- Anu Bradford, "International Antitrust: Negotiations and the False Hope of the WTO," *Harvard Journal of International Law* Volume 48, page 383 (2007)
- Oliver Budzinski, *The Governance of Global Competition: Competence Allocation in International Competition Policy* (2008)
- Sungjoon Cho et al. (eds.), *Competition Law on the Global Stage: David Gerber's Global Competition Law in Perspective* (2014)
- Maher M. Dabbah, *The Internationalization of Antitrust Policy* (2003)
- Josef Drexl, *The Future of Transnational Antitrust—From Comparative to Common Competition Law* (2007)
- Einar Elhauge and Damien Geradin, *Global Competition Law and Economics* (2nd ed, 2011)
- Eleanor M. Fox, "Toward World Antitrust and Market Access," *American Journal of International Law* Volume 91, Issue 1, page 1 (January 1997)

- Eleanor Fox and Michael J. Trebilcock, *The Design of Competition Law Institutions: Global Norms, Local Choices* (2013)
- Eleanor Fox and Daniel Crane, *Global Issues in Antitrust and Competition Law* (2nd ed., 2017)
- Tony Freyer, Antitrust and Global Capitalism, *1930–2004* (2006)
- David J. Gerber, "The European-U.S. Conflict Over the Globalization of Antitrust Law," *New England Law Review* Volume 34, page 123 (1999)
- David J. Gerber, *Global Competition: Law, Competition and Globalization* (2010)
- Andrew T. Guzman, "The Case for International Antitrust," *Berkeley Journal of International Law* Volume 22, page 355 (2004)
- Bernard Hoekman and Petros C. Mavroidis, "Economic Development, Competition Policy and the World Trade Organization," *Journal of World Trade* Volume 37, Issue 1, page 1 (2003)
- Kevin C. Kennedy, *Competition Law and the World Trade Organization: The Limits of Multilateralism* (2001)
- William Kovacic and Paulo Burnier da Silveira, *Global Competition Enforcement: New Players, New Challenges* (2019)
- John O. McGinnis, "The Political Economy of International Antitrust Harmonization," in Richard Epstein and Michael S. Greve (eds.), *Competition Laws in Conflict* (2004)
- Ralf Michaels, "Territorial Jurisdiction After Territoriality," in Piet Jan Slot and Mielle Bulterman (eds.), *Globalization and Jurisdiction* (2004)
- Chris Noonan, *The Emerging Principles of International Competition Law* (2008)
- Ronald J. Scott Jr., "International Development in a Complex Adaptive System," *Public Administration Quarterly* Volume 32, page 339 (2008)
- Daniel K. Tarullo, "Norms and Institutions in Global Competition Policy," *American Journal of International Law* Volume 94, page 478 (2000)
- Hanns Ulrich (ed.), *Comparative Competition Law: Approaching an International System of Antitrust Law* (1997)
- Spencer Weber Waller and Andre Fiebig, *Antitrust and American Business Abroad* (4th ed., 2015)

- Wyatt Wells, *Antitrust and the Formation of the Postwar World* (2002)
- Diane Wood, "Antitrust at the Global Level," *University of Chicago Law Review* Volume 72, page 309 (2005)

CHAPTER 12 CHALLENGES AND CHANGES

- Tembinkosi Bonakele, Eleanor M. Fox, and Liberty McClure, *Competition Policy for the New Era* (2017)
- David P. Cluchey, "Competition in Global Markets: Who Will Police the Giants," *Temple International and Comparative Law Journal* Volume 21, page 59 (2007)
- Ariel Ezrachi and Maurice Stucke, *Virtual Competition: The Promise and Perils of the Algorithm-Driven Economy* (2016)
- Stan J. Liebowitz and Stephen Margolis, *Winners, Losers and Microsoft: Competition and Antitrust in High Technology* (2001)
- Paul Lugard and Lee Roach, "The Era of Big Data and EU/U.S. Divergence for Refusals to Deal," *Antitrust* Volume 31, page 58 (2017)
- Mark R. Patterson, *Antitrust Law in the New Economy* (2017)
- Greg Sivinski et al., "Is Big Data a Big Deal? A Competition Law Approach to Big Data," *European Competition Journal* Volume 13, page 199 (2017)
- Maurice E. Stucke and Allen P. Grunes, *Big Data and Competition Policy* (2016)

INDEX